THE UNEXPLAINED

COMING FROM
THE SKIES

Produced by Carlton Books Limited
20 Mortimer Street
London, W1N 7RD

Text and Design copyright © Carlton Books Limited 2001

First published in hardback edition in 2001 by Chelsea House Publishers, a subsidiary of
Haights Cross Communications. Printed and bound in Dubai.

First Printing
1 3 5 7 9 8 6 4 2

The Chelsea House World Wide Web address is http://www.chelseahouse.com

Library of Congress Cataloging-in-Publication Data applied for

Historic Realms of Marvels and Miracles ISBN: 0-7910-6076-4
Ancient Worlds, Ancient Mysteries ISBN: 0-7910-6077-2
Lost Worlds and Forgotten Secrets ISBN: 0-7910-6078-0
We Are Not Alone ISBN: 0-7910-6079-9
Imagining Other Worlds ISBN: 0-7910-6080-2
Coming from the Skies ISBN: 0-7910-6081-0
Making Contact ISBN: 0-7910-6082-9

THE
UNEXPLAINED

COMING FROM
THE SKIES

Our Neighbors from Above

Hilary Evans

Chelsea House Publishers
Philadelphia

THE UNEXPLAINED

COMING FROM THE SKIES

CONTENTS

The Coming Of The UFOs

In 1947 it happened at last. For as long as anyone could remember, there had been talk about the Martians. There had been books, magazine stories, radio broadcasts. But on June 24, 1947, the maybes and the sometimes were suddenly right here and right now: fiction became fact, and dream became reality.

Or so it seemed. But was it, rather, that the world found the ingredients with which to create a new myth of otherworldly visitation? Was it more satisfying than the myth of ancient astronauts visiting the earth, because it was happening here and now, and more credible than the Star People (who maintain that they originate from other planets, and have been placed on earth for some higher purpose).

Whatever the facts of the matter, the coming of the saucers was a landmark event. Significantly, too, it was a media event. The term "flying saucer" was itself a media creation – a newspaperman's label – coined from the words used by pilot Kenneth Arnold to describe a formation of flying objects which he had not been able to identify while flying over the mountains of Washington state in June 1947.

Throughout the "Age of the Flying Saucer", which was born that day, the media would be in on the act – sometimes supportive of the believers, sometimes derisive, but always watching, commenting in a way that was not true of alleged extraterrestrial contacts that occurred before the era of the mass media. Previously, the people in the street had been largely indifferent to new views of the universe made possible by technological innovations even when they had been aware of them. Advances such as the invention of the telescope, then that of the balloon and, later, heavier-than-air flight, attracted little attention. In America, where the first controlled heavier-than-air flight was made by the Wright Brothers in 1903, there was almost total indifference to their achievement – so much so that the brothers, today two of the brightest stars in the American pantheon, took their invention to France.

The COMING
of the SAUCERS

By Kenneth Arnold & Ray Palmer

The cover of Arnold's book gives a false impression of how close the saucers were.

But with flying saucers, it was different. The media saw to it that the UFO phenomenon got coverage on an unprecedented scale, and this had significant repercussions for the phenomenon itself.

One fatal effect of media interest was to give the impression that UFOs, which are essentially a haphazard assortment of one-off anomalous events, constitute a phenomenon in its own right. Commentators, who like to have everyone and everything tidily classified and labelled, stuck the "flying saucer" label onto the assortment. This turned it into a category, with the result that anyone who sees anything strange in the sky is liable to ask "Is it a flying saucer? Is it a UFO?" Every time this happens, the witnesses make their own individual contribution to the communal myth.

This all-or-nothing approach, taking on board rubbish of every kind along with genuinely puzzling events, has meant that the UFO never achieved scientific recognition. The phenomenon ranges across the spectrum from fact to fantasy, incorporating Nazi bases under the Antarctic ice, mutilated cattle in the American mid-West, Men in Black knocking on the doors of witnesses, circular marks in cornfields interpreted as cosmic messages, malevolent Jinns, government conspiracies, abductees beamed up into spaceships for the purpose of inter-species breeding, and more. It's a rich and wonderful myth,

Fact or fiction? A typical flying saucer hovers above an unsuspecting human.

but it's not the stuff of which science is constructed. Yet it is important we bear in mind that, within the soft flesh of the myth, there remains a hard kernel of genuine scientific anomaly.

THE HISTORY OF THE UFO

We know now that UFOs did not suddenly start to appear on June 24, 1947. Of course there has never been a time when people did not see things in the sky they could not identify. In earlier chapters we saw how scattered puzzling observations provided historians of the subject with the material for a "prehistory" of the UFO. Periodically there have been clusters of reports which, while they are perhaps more easily accounted for in socio-cultural terms, have also been interpreted as flurries of extraterrestrial activity:

- There was a wave of sightings of mystery airships across the United States during the 1890s. This was at a time when experimentation with flying machines was widespread, and the competition to be the first to achieve controlled flight was feverish. But there were no airships flying in the American skies which could have accounted for the sightings.
- Other airship scares followed, notably in Britain just before World War One. At this time, general apprehension of the imminent hostilities was symbolized by Germany's Zeppelin, a sinister menace which seemed more threatening as war loomed closer. There were so many "sightings" that the popular alarm provoked anxious questions in the British Parliament. Similar scares took place in New Zealand.
- A wave of more than 1000 sightings of "mystery aircraft" was reported from Scandinavia during the 1930s, often observed flying in conditions which at the time were considered impossible. This was a time when rearmament was contributing to

The 1965 book, UFOs, Nazi Secret Weapon, *capitalized on the idea that the Nazis had developed all manner of mystery aircraft. It is known that they had built a prototype of a saucer-shaped craft.*

international tension, and international tension was inspiring further rearmament, and when both Nazi Germany and Soviet Russia represented unknown potential threats.

- In the tense postwar summer of 1946, a time that was made uneasy by the Cold War, some 1600 reports were made of "ghost rockets" hurtling through the skies of Scandinavia.

THE AGE OF THE FLYING SAUCER

But Arnold's 1947 sighting – and the "Age of the Flying Saucer" that it ushered in – were rarely seen in the perspective of these former manifestations, as part of a continuing phenomenon. As far as the public was concerned, flying saucers were something totally new and altogether without parallel. Whether they were welcomed as friendly visitors bearing greetings from other inhabited parts of the universe or feared as alien invaders, it soon came to be taken for granted that their occupants were of extraterrestrial origin. The terms "flying saucer" and "alien spacecraft" became interchangeable.

This is not to say that the world rushed headlong into the idea that these things came from beyond Earth. Other possibilities were seriously considered – in particular, that the objects were secret military devices of the Americans or the Russians. As American researcher Martin Kottmeyer has pointed out:

> Polls from 1947 into the Sixties show the secret weapons idea had clear dominance in the minds of the general public. One from 1968 showed 57% thought most UFOs were due to secret defense projects either in the U.S. or another country. Only 40% thought people were seeing space ships from another planet.

More than one theory was derived from the military experiments of German scientists, who were known to have developed a saucer-shaped aircraft at least to prototype stage. An elaborate theory, backed with persuasive fact, was developed by the Italian writer Renato Vesco. His conclusion was that the flying saucers should be credited to the British and Canadian governments, who had developed secret disc-shaped devices based on German wartime research. An equally impressive array of circumstantial evidence was produced by Germans in Canada, making out a strong alternative scenario in which the Nazi scientists escaped from Germany after World War Two to previously prepared bases in the Antarctic.

Both explanations were plausible, and pointed to a substantial body of suggestive if circumstantial evidence. Other theories moved from the possible, through the improbable, to the bizarre. One school of thought suggested that the UFO occupants were travelling in time – that they were actually our own descendants and had come to look at their ancestors. Another popular line was religious, and stated that UFOs were vehicles carrying demons. With such a wealth of alleged sightings of every shape, size and configuration, there is hardly any limit to the scenarios that can be constructed if the ingredients are carefully selected. Some years ago, a UFO periodical invited readers to submit UFO explanations that no one believed in. So strong a case can be made that the UFOs are sent by occult Masters of Wisdom hidden in the Himalayas that I almost convinced myself! Other such theories were put forward seriously, and the books are there to prove it: *Flying Saucers from the Fourth Dimension* (Kurt Glemser, 1969); *God Drives a Flying Saucer* (R L Dione, 1969); *Flying Saucers from the Earth's interior* (Raymond Bernard, 1958).

One by one, though, these alternative scenarios were set aside – largely because there was no real evidence for them. Yet, ironically, nor was there any evidence for the scenario that came to predominate – the extraterrestrial hypothesis that flying saucers came from other worlds. So long as the flying saucers were objects seen afar, there seemed no way of resolving the

Alleged alien remains from the 1948 crash of a flying saucer near Aztec, New Mexico.

question. If only we could meet their occupants, though, that would settle the matter. The world waited for the moment when a flying saucer would land on the White House lawn and Little Green Men would step out and say to the nearest bystander, "Take me to your leader!" Or, if the flying saucer occupants were reluctant to initiate a voluntary meeting, perhaps one would make a forced landing, or even crash.

THE SAUCER CRASHES

One of the more bizarre aspects of the UFO phenomenon is the rumour that a flying saucer has crashed, and that it – together with the bodies of its occupants – is being held in secret by the United States Government.

Stories of crashed UFOs began to be told almost as soon as the idea of "flying saucers" became prevalent. At one time or another, saucers have been said to have crashed in Spitzbergen (1952), Heligoland (1955), Mexico (1948, 1950 and 1964), Bolivia (1978) and in various locations in south-west United States – Salinas, California (1947), Aztec, New Mexico (1948) and elsewhere. Each of these stories created a flurry of interest at the time, then faded when no confirming evidence was forthcoming. Some may have been deliberate hoaxes, others rumours and misinterpretations.

Then, in the 1970s, the subject was revived when veteran American investigator Leonard Stringfield began to collect statements from individuals who claimed to have been involved in official investigation of crashed saucers in the late 1940s. In a series of dossiers, he brought together dozens of personal stories which, though they were mostly circumstantial, nearly always anonymous, frequently contradictory, nevertheless converged towards a common theme. They said that a flying saucer had crashed in a desert area in south-west United States, that alien bodies – and perhaps even survivors – had been recovered, and that the crashed discs, together with their occupants, had been taken away by the authorities for top secret examination and analysis.

ROSWELL

In 1980 Berlitz and Moore published *The Roswell Incident*, which offered evidence that complemented Stringfield's findings and, moreover, focussed on a specific time and place. The time was July 1947 – that is to say, within weeks of Kenneth Arnold's landmark sighting; the place, Roswell, New Mexico. In the words of the jacket blurb:

> … after extensive research and considerable detective work, Charles Berlitz and William Moore have pieced together the strongest evidence to date that a manned UFO actually reached earth – over thirty years ago!

The head and torso of a replica alien on an autopsy table. The "alien" is an exhibit at the International UFO Museum and Research Center in Roswell.

Two "Aliens" watching the the comet Hale-Bopp in the night sky over Roswell. Many inhabitants of the town still believe that aliens landed in the area in 1947.

But by now the story had acquired sufficient momentum to keep going despite all criticism. It was admitted that not all the testimony was reliable, but that was only to be expected when half a century had elapsed and many of those who had participated in the events were no longer alive to testify.

While most versions of the myth were honest attempts to uncover the truth, some of the variations were curious, not to say bizarre. Perhaps the most remarkable was the story told by a senior US Army officer of high repute, Philip Corso, in 1997. He confirms the basic fact, that an extraterrestrial craft crashed in the desert near Roswell, adding that he himself saw physical evidence of it. Further, he describes in seeming detail how he was personally responsible for the handling of much of the debris from the crash, which he was instructed to pass on to selected commercial companies for the purposes of "back-engineering". We are asked to believe that, as a direct result of analysing the scraps of wreckage strewn about the Roswell desert, several important breakthroughs were achieved that significantly accelerated the progress of technological research. The laser, micro-circuits, fibre optics and night-vision devices are just four of the applications the author mentions.

Doubters were quick to point out the glaring improbabilities, inconsistencies and outright impossibilities of Corso's story, but this only fuelled the mystery. How did so senior an officer, of hitherto unblemished reputation, come to be publishing this nonsense? What authorization, if any, did he have to go public with these revelations? Deliberate hoax? Fiction pretending to be fact? The truth has yet to be revealed, but the real importance of Corso's claim is to show how, by absorbing the facts, twisting them, stretching them, and extrapolating from them, the mythmakers feed and fatten the myth.

In fact, the actual events were much simpler than the mythical scenario, and not nearly so exciting. There was indeed a "crash" at Roswell, in the sense that something came down from the skies. What came down was a weather balloon, which would have come down somewhere, sooner or later, in any case.

The extraordinary legend that then grew up is a magnificent example of myth-making in action. The starting-point was that there was no starting-point. No official record of the incident, no government documents whatever, were known to exist. At the same time, there could be little doubt that *something* had come down from the sky near Roswell in July 1947, that the authorities were well aware of this, and that some kind of official action had been taken. In the initial confusion, an official press release was unquestionably issued, announcing the crash of a "flying saucer". Though it was retracted a day or two later, it was enough to set rumours flying. Gradually, the few known facts were embellished. Witnesses were found and scenarios were constructed, until something approaching a consensus history of the event was created, along with a shelf-full of book-length treatments proposing individual perspectives on the basic theme.

Critics pointed out that no two versions of the story matched. The witnesses contradicted one another, and sometimes themselves, and many of the allegations could not have been true, if only because they were incompatible.

An artist's impression of the flying saucer that allegedly crashed during a thunder storm at Roswell on July 2, 1947.
The next day many pieces of debris were found on a sheep farm nearby.

It was of a secret type which, because it might be used for espionage over other countries that might not appreciate it, had to be kept from public knowledge.

How did a weather balloon come to be announced as a flying saucer? This was unquestionably the result of the prevailing emotional climate. The Arnold sighting had sparked off a wave of interest world-wide just weeks before, and during those first months, before a more realistic assessment could be made, thousands of sightings were reported. The Roswell "crash" occurred while all over the United States people were reporting seeing the mysterious "flying saucers". Every unknown object was liable to be perceived as a saucer, and the thing that came down at Roswell was an "unknown". With the benefit of hindsight, it can be seen that those responsible over-reacted and rushed to premature judgement, but

given the mood of the time, their mistake is not so surprising.

Another aspect of the Roswell phenomenon is the way in which the myth was sustained in the face of continued official denial. Government sources, by making it obvious that something was being concealed, gave free rein to the amateur theorists to claim that a cover-up – if not a conspiracy – was in progress, and this was, in a sense, true. Scores of theorists went into action, producing article after article, book after book. It is significant of the crash stories – and we shall see that the same is true of contactees and abductees – that most of the revelations are made not, as should be the case, by official pronouncement or authoritative statement, but by individuals writing books sold by commercial publishers. Under such circumstances, it should not be expected that a neutral, honest

presentation of the facts will take place. A large part of the Roswell controversy consists of rival theorists bashing one another's claims.

The town of Roswell itself is thriving on the myth. A substantial income is derived from tourism, and two museums attract visitors from all over the world. Though its present notoriety is unlikely to endure, Roswell has earned its place in history. But if so, it will not be as the place where the aliens landed, but as the location for one of the classic legends, along with Loch Ness and Lourdes. Neither Roswell, nor any of the other stories of crashed saucers, offer any evidence whatsoever of visitation from other worlds. Rather, they demonstrate what happens when the myth-making process is allowed to follow its own course, unhampered by inconvenient fact.

FLYING SAUCERS FROM OUTER SPACE

The astonishing fact is that there is not a scrap of evidence for the otherworldly origin of UFOs. The popular conception whereby they have come to be perceived as extraterrestrial spaceships is supported by nothing but conjecture.

However, it has to be said that the conjecture is a perfectly logical one. If UFOs are truly behaving as witnesses say they are, there is nothing on Earth that can behave in that way, so it makes sense to suppose that their origin is elsewhere. The weak point in that argument is, of course, the question of whether UFOs are truly behaving as witnesses claim. In his 1979 work *The UFO Handbook*, American investigator Allan Hendry showed how easily an honest and well-intentioned witness can misinterpret what is seen:

- A witness who saw a balloon said "it looked like the saucers you read about".
- A witness who watched a star for an hour said "it made a whirring noise".
- A witness described an advertising plane as "something out of *Star Wars*".
- A woman scared by an ad plane screamed for her husband to get back in the car.
- A witness who saw Venus and Mars for a whole week said she was "scared so bad, could hardly breathe [and] lost sleep".
- Police officers who saw stars said they had "never seen anything like it all of our lives".
- A woman who watched a star changing colour over a period of hours thought "Oh my Lord, it's the end of the world! I'd better get down on my knees and pray!"

Hendry's findings reveal a phenomenon well known to researchers; that there are virtually no limits to how people will reclassify what they see to

The triangle shaped UFOs that were observed by many people over the outskirts of Brussels.

match what they expect to see. In fact, the history of the UFO phenomenon is largely a chronicle of things turning out to not be what they seem. From the start, it was recognized that at least nine out of ten of the cases reported turned out to have some explanation – sometimes prosaic, sometimes truly bizarre. Sometimes, too, the explanation was on the secret list. There is no doubt that clandestine aviation developments would have

explained a number of sightings, if they had been public knowledge. For example, a massive wave of sightings was reported over Belgium in 1989. On November 29, 150 eyewitness reports came from the small town of Eupen alone. Even making allowance for excited imaginations, there seems no doubt that the sightings, 2000 or more in all, related to some unknown object overflying the country. Since its behaviour was unlike that of any known

aircraft, many believed they had no choice but to ascribe the sightings to something out of this world.

The only viable alternative was that the Americans were testing secret aircraft over one of the most densely populated places in the world. Could they really be so stupid as to do anything so dangerous? It is hard to believe, yet investigation shows that this is the least improbable of all the explanations offered.

June 1966: an experimental disc made by Paul Villa to a design that he claims was offered to him by visiting aliens from Coma Berneices.

THE VARIETY OF UFOS

Once the idea had been accepted that flying saucers might come from beyond Earth, it quickly became the explanation of choice, until for the majority of people, flying saucers – and later UFOs – came to be a synonym for extraterrestrial spacecraft. It was the simplest scenario, because it was simply a transposition of our own first tentative ventures beyond our own atmosphere. The simplicity was deceptive, however. The moment the claims were seriously evaluated, problems came thick and fast.

In the first place, there was the fact that hardly any two UFOs looked alike. Investigators did their best to prepare charts of the various kinds, much as, during World War Two, charts of aircraft types had been prepared for spotters. The diversity of descriptions was so great however that only a proportion could be fitted into any pre-prepared pigeonhole. Hundreds of sightings were one-of-a-kind events, defying classification. How could one make sense of this variety? One way was to break them down in terms of size and function:

- the very small ones – too small to contain a human-size occupant – were perceived as probes, unmanned, remote-controlled information-gatherers. Paul Villa claimed to have photographed some of these near Albuquerque, New Mexico in the 1960s.
- small discs, which might be the equivalent of a private motor car, were perceived as "scouts". They were certainly manned, because occupants were sometimes seen, as in the 1970 Cowichan case.
- larger discs, often described as being about 20 metres (65 ft) in diameter, were probably the most frequently reported, even though they varied greatly in appearance. The sighting at Helena, Montana 1966, was a classic instance of this classic configuration.
- cigar-shaped craft, resembling airships – often described as very big – were perceived as "mother ships". These did not themselves come close to the Earth's surface. Instead, they housed "scout ships" which emerged and came closer to the ground. George Adamski claimed to have photographed some of these, together with their scouts.
- finally, there were the truly massive UFOs, often said to be "the size of a football field". A group of witnesses in 1977 at Partington, Lancashire, described the object they saw in these terms, although one of them compared it to a floating restaurant.

This rough-and-ready classification made sense when related to our own

A classic domed disk with windows and four-piece landing gear hovers over a house in Helena, Montana. The "flying saucer" was reportedly seen in April 1966.

A UFO magazine from 1977 depicting a huge cigar-shaped extraterrestrial craft crashing down to Earth.

Earth methods. When the time came for us to start exploring space, the first ventures would be made with unmanned "probes". The first manned spacecraft were very small, carrying one astronaut. As technology developed they grew larger, carrying more passengers and equipment. But should this logical development be applied to spacecraft from other worlds? If so, it presupposed not only that the aliens would go about things in the same way that we did, but that they themselves were pretty much the same size as us, and similar to us in many other respects.

THE OCCUPANTS

In much the same way as our ideas about their technology altered, our ideas of otherworldly beings also changed over time. Even as late as the 1930s, science fiction writers and artists were contemplating all kinds of monsters varying from the human norm in almost every conceivable respect. What a relief it was to find, when the first sightings were made of flying saucer occupants, that they were not so very different from ourselves:

- Near Hopkinsville, Kentucky, on the night of August 21, 1955, the Sutton farming family found themselves "besieged" by a group of short humanoid creatures, about 1 metre tall. They had the oversized heads so frequently reported, very long arms and huge, taloned hands. The eyes were large and glowing, and their bodies had a silver metallic appearance, though whether this was flesh or clothing, the terrified witnesses could not be sure.
- At Socorro, on April 24, 1964, American police patrolman Lonnie Zamora saw a landed UFO. Nearby were "two small figures in what resembled white coveralls ... they appeared normal. Small though – maybe the size of boys".

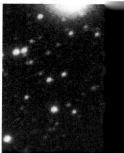

- On July 1, 1965, French lavender farmer Maurice Masse had a very similar experience when he arrived at his fields near Valensole. A UFO the shape of a rugby ball was standing among his bushes. Nearby was a human being of the height and build of a child of about eight ... wearing a one-piece suit, but no helmet. Inside the machine I could see another being. ... the one who was down on the ground ... saw me, and he immediately jumped into the machine.

EXOBIOLOGY

July 1, 1965: working early in the morning in his lavender field Maurice Masse came across an alien craft and its occupants.

Exobiology – the study of the biology of extraterrestrials – is about as far from being an exact science as it is possible to get. There is indeed no certainty that there is any actual material for the science to study. The data are all derived from witness testimony, and the evaluation is wholly speculative. It amounts to little more than academic game-playing, albeit with a serious underlying intention.

Exobiologists necessarily take as their starting point the fact that the visiting aliens seem to adapt very readily to Earth's environment. Though this may seem "natural", it is really somewhat astonishing. It implies, for example, that they do not find our planet either too cold or too hot, though we know that temperatures on the planets of the Solar System vary enormously. Even here on Earth, many people find it difficult to adapt to Saharan heat or Polar cold. Again, they breathe our atmosphere quite happily, adjusting to it more easily than Earthpeople do to the rarefied air of, say, the Peruvian uplands. They do not seem to be troubled by whatever level of humidity they encounter, though most Earthpeople find our own jungle or rainforest conditions extremely difficult to cope with.

Is it simply that we are less adaptable than our alien visitors, or do they indeed come from a planet exactly like our own? Perhaps they are much less sensitive than we are to minor differences in environmental conditions. Perhaps they are wearing protective clothing which compensates for any difference. Or maybe the beings we meet are not the aliens in their true form, but in a form adopted for the specific purpose of visiting Earth, and therefore adapted to it. Whether any of these or any other explanations are valid, the paradox of alien compatibility is not easily accounted for.

But that is not the only paradox of alien appearance – there is also the problem of their variety. In a 1966

Later he added that the alien, on becoming aware of him, immobilized him with a hand-held tubular device before re-entering the UFO.

Although there were many variations, the flying saucer occupants encountered in these three cases are typical of the first close encounter stories. Clearly, they could not be mistaken for humans. Equally clearly though, they were not monsters.

We had no reason to suppose that this would be the case. In principle, extraterrestrial visitors could just as well be very much smaller or very much larger than we are. There is no reason to suppose that conditions on other worlds are anything like our own, but even if we assume that this is so, even very minor differences would affect the appearance of its residents. Our own Earth supports beings as varied as the ant and the elephant, the shrimp and the whale.

A great many science fiction plots involve non-human creatures with human or even superhuman intelligence. Giant ants are a Hollywood favourite, and all kinds of creatures have at one time or another been recruited to send shivers down sci-fi readers' spines. Suppose we set these aside and make the assumption – which we have really

no right to make – that only creatures fundamentally similar to ourselves, bipedal, walking rather than crawling or swimming, with brains contained in bony cases at the top of a spinal column, and so on, have been endowed with the necessary mental equipment to start exploring space. Even so, that still leaves open a wide variety of options. A very small difference in gravity could lead to marked differences in size. Differences in light would affect sense organs, so that visiting aliens might find Earth blindingly bright or gloomily obscure. Differences in atmospheric make-up would lead to different-sized breathing organs, and so on. Unless our visitors came from a planet precisely made up like ours, we should expect them to differ in appearance to a greater or lesser degree.

Which, of course, they do. Paradoxically, though, the appearance of alien visitors, as described by witnesses, does not involve differences which can clearly be attributed to environmental differences. Knowing how our own biological parameters are dictated by our environment, we ought to be able to infer, from the appearance of visiting aliens, what conditions prevail on their home planet. But no clear indications of this sort have hitherto emerged.

RIGHT: *Through the looking glass: the basically humanoid features of a "short gray" alien.*

The massive head and huge "wrap-around" eyes of the stereotypical Short-Gray alien as identified by the writer-researcher Patrick Huyghe.

conditioned our own structure. In short, they conclude, "this creature will be basically like an ape, a human, or, perhaps, the frequently reported little men observed in connection with UFO sightings".

In fact, descriptions of UFO occupants vary as much as the descriptions of the craft themselves. In Patrick Huyghe's authoritative *Field Guide to Extraterrestrials*, by far the largest section comprises bipedal beings more or less similar to ourselves. The remaining sections – Animalian, Robotic and Exotic – have markedly fewer specimens. All the varieties he presents are taken from actual cases, but this is precisely the weakness of attempting any such classification. The "identikit" drawings are artist drawings made from descriptions – sometimes verbal, sometimes witness' sketches. They are subject to all the shortcomings of eye-witness testimony – faulty observation, misinterpretation, defects of memory, the tendency to rationalize and to replace the unknown with the known. Moreover, the great majority of the more exotic varieties rest on the testimony of a single witness. Most aliens were seen on one occasion only, by a solitary individual.

That aliens should vary so much in appearance is even more surprising than that the UFOs should vary. After all, our aircrews use a wide variety of aircraft for different purposes, but the people who fly them are roughly similar. Are we receiving visitors from a great number of different worlds? Or do many different races live on the worlds that visit us, with great physical differences between them?

The situation is not simplified by the fact that some stereotypes have emerged. You will have noticed that in the three cases I mentioned earlier – Zamora, Masse and the Sutton family – the aliens were all short humanoids, with a tendency to have large heads. This style of alien gradually evolved – so far as Earth witnesses are concerned – into the type which Huyghe labels "Short Gray". Originally reported by the abductees Barney and Betty Hill, whose adventure we shall consider in the next chapter, this has become – with minor variations – a stereotype for abductees. They are fundamentally

magazine article, Jack and Mary Robinson outlined the basic requirements for an intelligent alien being, showing that the most probable type would be carbon-based rather than silicon or crystalline-based. It would also have a hydrogen-oxygen cycle as opposed to chlorine-fluorine-methane or a hydrogen-fluorine cycle, both of which, whatever their advantages as a source of energy, would have seriòus drawbacks in terrestrial environmental conditions. Consequently, they argue, any alien capable of surviving on Earth would have, basically, to conform to the same parameters as those which have human in appearance, with two legs, two arms, trunk and head. The major differences are the very large head and the big black "wrap-around" eyes. The nose, mouth and ears are optional. If the beings are naked there is no indication of navel or genitals. The number of fingers and toes may vary, but by and large the Short Grays barely fall outside the parameters of human appearance.

Does this mean that we can say that – setting aside the countless variations – we do have, in the Short Grays, an identifiable alien species? Unfortunately, this is not particularly realistic. For the differences between them, though minor, are none the less very real. We might try to set them aside by blaming defective observation – the witnesses, in the excitement of the encounter, might well have mistaken a detail like a nose or ears. But we are still left with the problem of working out which version is the correct one.

There is always a further possibility, that of confabulation: that witnesses are seeing what they expect to see, and what they expect to see will be based on what others have seen. For example, researcher Nick Pope mentions the case of "Mary", an Irish abductee:

> Mary saw a copy of Whitley Strieber's book, *Communion*, and stopped in her tracks. The artist's impression of Whitley's alien, which was on the front cover of the book, was identical to the fairy that she had seen all those years ago. It was this incident that first caused her to suspect that some of the incidents from her childhood might not be due to fairies after all.

While at first sight such cases seem to have a literal interpretation – that seeing the artist's depiction of Strieber's entity reminded Mary of the entity she had herself seen but forgotten – there is also the possibility that she was responding to an archetype which was embedded in her subconscious. Though this sounds far-fetched, it conforms to the patterns of human behaviour pioneered by researchers, notably the eminent Swiss psychologist Carl Jung, who made a study of the subject and wrote a book entitled *Flying Saucers: A Modern Myth of Things Seen in the Skies* (1958).

ALIEN AGGRESSORS

Reports of UFOs run into millions; reports of their occupants into thousands. But when it comes to working out what those occupants do, what their intentions are, and why they are here, we have very little useful to go on. All information comes from the contact and abduction cases that we shall look at more closely in the next chapter.

Yet if the alien visitations are genuine, they must have a purpose. Simply to know that purpose would be an immense step forward in our understanding of the universe. Are otherworldly beings driven by the same motivations as ourselves, or are their actions governed by a wholly different agenda, one which we might never understand, even if we were told?

Our own thinking as to why beings from one world should visit other worlds has been dominated by two ideas, one positive and the other negative. On the one hand, we have scientific curiosity and exploration; on the other, aggression, invasion, and domination. Writer Jules Verne in his famous science fiction works published in the late 1800s, portrayed space travellers on a strictly scientific mission of exploration. H.G. Wells, however, in his famous story *The War of the Worlds*, portrayed both his Selenites and his Martians as dangerous, and he set the pattern for most subsequent writers. It is true to say that the vast majority of science fiction, when dealing with interaction between ourselves and the extraterrestrials, involves conflict to a greater or lesser extent. Even that great television series, *Star Trek*, had an on-going hostility with the Klingons as a background to incidents which all too often involved some kind of armed confrontation.

So, when the Flying Saucers came, suspicion was uppermost in most people's minds. Brad Steiger, who strangely enough identified himself in later years as one of the "Star People" who came from outer space to live among humans, co-wrote two books in the 1960s describing UFOs as anything but benign. *Flying Saucers are Hostile*

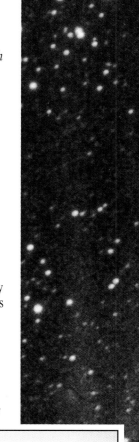

and *Flying Saucer Invasion: Target Earth* both written with Joan Whritenour) must have sowed unease about these extraterrestrial visitors:

> There is a wealth of well-documented evidence that UFOs have been responsible for murders, assaults, burnings with direct-ray focus, radiation sickness, kidnappings, pursuits of automobiles, attacks on homes, disruptions of power sources, paralysis, mysterious cremations, and destruction of aircraft.

By contrast, the French group GABRIEL, in their wide-ranging survey of the phenomenon, found only six cases of alien aggression. One took place in 1897, where a Michigan farmer was hit by a "Martian"; three related cases occurred in Venezuela, where the testimony of the young men concerned is open to question; a 1958 case at Hoganas, Sweden, involved an attack by

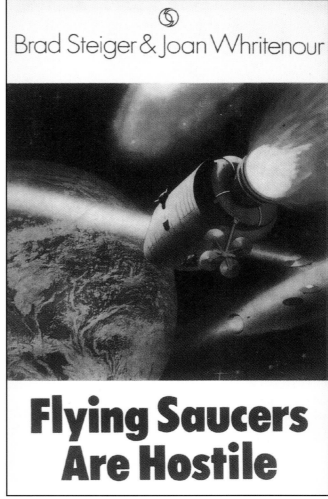

Brad Steiger & Joan Whritenour

Flying Saucers Are Hostile

Steiger and Whritenour's book in which UFOs are perceived as aggressive invaders.

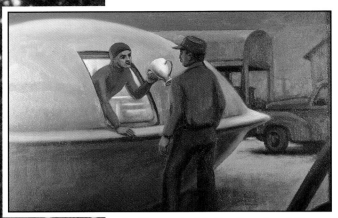

Joe Simonton is visited by aliens who ask him for some water; in return they give him pancakes.

"fluid" creatures who fled when a motor-horn was sounded; and a 1965 case from Argentina involved three schoolboys, and no UFO was sighted.

If that is the worst we have to fear, it is hard to take General MacArthur's 1955 warning seriously: "The nations of the world will have to unite, for the next war will be an interplanetary war". Forty years on, we can be thankful that no war of the worlds has broken out, no alien invasion has taken place. The only aspect of alien behaviour which can be construed as aggressive is the habit of abducting humans and subjecting them to medical examination pattern. Even that is seen as benevolent by many commentators.

ALIEN CURIOSITY

As we have seen, even Brad Steiger changed his mind about the aliens and came to think of them as benevolent. Most researchers have dismissed the aggression stories as exaggerated: though we don't know what they do mean, it doesn't seem as though they mean us harm. But that only makes it harder to understand what motivates them. Most of the time they simply fly overhead. They wave at Father Gill and his flock at Papua New Guinea in June 1959. In April 1961, they present Joe Simonton with four pancakes. At Cennina, Italy, in November 1954, two of them grab Rosa Lotti's flowers and try to take her stockings. At Vilvorde, Belgium, in 1973, a metre- (3-ft) high humanoid seems to be examining a suburban garden with something like a

metal detector. Simple aggression we could understand, but most of their behaviour is ambiguous to the point of absurdity, and disentangling a motive has not been easy. That hasn't stopped a lot of people from making a guess, though.

The default scenario must be that the aliens are simply curious, just as our own space exploration is motivated largely by scientific curiosity. Yet, though this may seem to us the most plausible motive, there is little evidence to support it. Occasionally sightings are reported in which the aliens are seen apparently collecting soil samples, but if that's what they are doing, they do

not seem to be going about it very enthusiastically. There are no signs of any methodical exploration, such as we make on our own expeditions to the Moon and Mars. No alien has ever been seen using a camera, a theodolite, or even a tape measure …

The most evident indications of scientific curiosity seem to be the abduction reports, where examinations of human physiology, the taking of sperm samples and so on suggest a biological interest. But, there are serious problems with the abductees' testimony. In any case it raises the question that if the aliens are indeed motivated by scientific curiosity, is it reasonable that

Rosa Lotti ,an Italian housewife, encountered aliens while she was walking through the woods to church in 1954. The aliens grabbed the flowers she was holding and tried to take her stockings!

the only form that curiosity takes is examining the bodies of abducted humans? Why do they seem to show no interest in our engineering achievements, our cities, our monuments? Do they have so many pyramids of their own that they won't spare ours a glance?

But the moment we use a word like "reasonable", we are reminded how little we have the right to impose our notions of what is reasonable on these otherworldly beings. Particularly when we don't even know for sure that they exist.

HERE TO HELP US

The best way to understand the aliens' motives would be to have them tell us in their own words. According to those who claim to have met them, they are often happy to do this. Gloria Lee, a famous alien contactee, quotes her extraterrestrial contact, J.W. from Jupiter:

> We have come to your planet to help with your evolvement ... We bring you the way to a new life. We can help your planet immensely with the knowledge in our possession. We come in peace and brotherly love.

The great majority of the contactees we shall be considering in the following chapter insist that the aliens they meet have benevolent intentions. Hundreds of books have been written, recording messages obtained from these beings either by channeling, dictation or automatic writing. They tend to share the same message – inviting Earthpeople to qualify for Cosmic Brotherhood by learning to live in peace and love, caring for the environment, giving up war, and the like. The general principles are fine, but unfortunately they are not accompanied by any practical advice on how they are to be realized. The fact that they are given to people who are not in any position to implement them is also regrettable. Random members of the general public, however enthusiastic, are not likely to bring wars to an end.

On a more immediately practical level, there have been, throughout the history of the UFO phenomenon, reports of individuals being healed by the UFO occupants. A Canadian lady told me she received daily visits from aliens who were actively co-operating with the Mexican Government to find a cure for cancer. American author Preston Dennett collected more than 100 cases in his book *UFO Healings*. The author admits to having previously been skeptical about UFOs, but became convinced of their existence due to the number of cases in which individuals claim to have been healed thanks to alien intervention. Picking one case at random, we read how Licia Davidson of Los Angeles, who had been having UFO contacts for as long as she can remember, was in 1989 diagnosed as having terminal cancer and given three months to live. Soon after, she was abducted by aliens who operated on her. The next time she visited her doctor, all traces of her cancer had gone.

The cases quoted by Dennett cover a wide range of ailments, and a variety of treatments are used by the alien doctors. Some 30% of patients are healed with more-or-less conventional surgery, 21% with a beam of light, 13% with unfamiliar instruments, 9% with pills, salves or other medication, and 5% by "alien mind power". A good many take place on board UFOs. Others receive their healing either while observing a UFO – usually in the form of a beam of light – or in the course of house visits by aliens.

There are even cases where some kind of "absent healing" seems to occur. A particularly puzzling case is that of an American woman, Beryl Hendricks. Beryl was at home one day in 1978 when she joined her husband on a couch. There, she appeared to pass out. It seemed to her that she was on some kind of operating table, with a number of figures around her. They removed a tumour from her breast.

During the whole of this time she was watched by her husband, however. He saw that she did not move from the couch. In other words, the operation did not take place in physical reality. Yet, if we can believe her subsequent claim, the operation was actually performed, and the tumour was really and truly gone when she woke. Psychologist Kenneth Ring, who investigated the case, was baffled. Though no believer in UFOs, he asked "What on earth – or in heaven – do we have here? Is this a Near Death Experience or some kind of UFO encounter?"

If we accept the physical reality of extraterrestrial visitors, we are obliged to credit them with the healing. Besides the cases collected by Dennett, many others have been recorded from all parts of the world. However, we should bear in mind that preoccupation with our physical health not only plays a large part in our daily life, but is intimately bound up with our beliefs. For instance, healing is a recurrent theme in Christian religious belief. Jesus himself is credited with many healings, and a healing miracle, either during the person's life or as a result of a pilgrimage visit to a shrine, is virtually essential for any candidate for sainthood.

This does not invalidate healings by extraterrestrial visitors, but it does require us to consider them in the wider

Gloria Lee, founder of the Cosmon Foundation, who starved herself to death on alien's instructions.

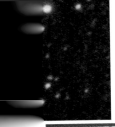

The fairy Melsuine, who, once her true nature was discovered by her husband, resumed her fairy shape and left him.

context that all visitors from other worlds – except those specifically evil or hostile – are credited with healing. This is tantamount to saying that they are expected to perform healings. Any visitor from another world who carries a cure for cancer in his briefcase can be sure of an immediate welcome.

To counter skepticism, the medical authorities at Lourdes now require very strict evidence for a healing miracle attributable to Bernadette's vision of Mary. At the very least, they require thorough medical documentation of the patient's state both before and after. The sick who go to Lourdes, knowing this, can make sure ahead of their visit that such records are available, because they go there in deliberate hope of a cure. But UFO-related healings come out of the blue. Because the patient is taken by surprise, it is rare that satisfactory documentation is available.

This is true even of the best-documented instance, the classic case of "Dr X". On November 2 at 4 o'clock in the morning, he saw, from the terrace of his home, a pair of linked UFOs unlike any reported elsewhere. They directed a beam at him, then left with a loud bang. He woke his wife, who noted that an

ankle wound, sustained three days before while chopping wood, had gone. The next day, he found himself cured of a war injury, which had for years partially paralysed his right arm and leg. He also had a strange triangular mark on his belly, and so did his 14-month son.

Although investigated by Aimé Michel, France's most eminent ufologist, the case rests largely on the say-so of the witness. Taken at face value, it implies that the occupants of two UFOs, knowing of Dr X's predicament, made a special journey to his neighbourhood, carried out various manoeuvres, then directed a beam at him which instantly cured both a paralysis and a physical injury, besides other effects. In other words, the supposed beam of light somehow transferred to Dr X's body the equivalent of medication. It performed manipulation if not surgery, provided whatever was needed for instant regeneration of tissue, and so on … This is aside from diagnosing the complaints in the first place. Some beam of light! If this is what actually took place, then the cure is as miraculous as any reported in a religious context.

Another disconcerting case occurred in 1984. *The Weekly World News* told how Australian yachtsman Steve Palmer, sailing in the Bermuda Triangle, was too sick with an infected appendix even to sail to shore, though he knew he needed urgent treatment. Fortunately, a ball of white light appeared in the sky, changing into a trio of two-metre (6-ft) tall men in metallic green bodysuits. He fell asleep, and when he woke, the aliens told him his appendix was gone into the sea. They cooked him a warm white broth to recover his strength. There was a surgical incision on his right side. When he got back to the Bahamas, a doctor told him he had had a professional appendectomy done on him within the past 2–4 days.

The absence of convincing medical records for these alien healings is doubly unfortunate. If we could be certain that they did really take place as claimed by the patient, we would know for sure that the extraterrestrial visitors exist on the same plane of reality as ourselves, able to operate in the material world that we inhabit. Moreover, we would know that their intentions are benevolent.

SEX WITH ALIENS

Romances between humans and otherworldly beings are a traditional feature of legend. Mermaids, in particular, have a distressing habit of falling in love with humans, leading to difficulties – often fatal – when it becomes a question of "My place or yours?" Frequently such stories involve the Cupid and Psyche motif, whereby one must not see the other, or utter their name, or so on. The fairy Melusine was just one of many creatures whose relationship with a human came to an sad end for this reason. When she was forced to leave, her husband retained custody of their children, though she came to revisit them at night when he and their new stepmother were asleep.

The question of whether humans can have sexual relations with aliens obviously depends on how human-like they are. This brings us back to the questions we had to consider earlier in this book. If there is to be crossbreeding between aliens and ourselves, they must be genetically similar to us. Dr Michael Swords, in an article entitled "Extraterrestrial Hybridization Unlikely", has pointed out the biological obstacles. Inter-species breeding is a virtual impossibility because each species has different numbers of chromosomes – the numbers range from 2 to 200. There is no record of successful mating between humans (with 23 pairs of chromosomes per cell) and gorillas or chimpanzees (with 24), so the aliens would need to be even closer to us than the apes.

The basic chemistry of all life on Earth is extremely complex, and it is specifically adapted to conditions on our planet. Even if life were to develop on another planet in exactly the same way as it did on Earth – itself an astronomically unlikely chance – all the components would need to be the same. Suppose we assume that coincidence, it would still be necessary for those ingredients to be present in the same proportions, and to match in number and arrangement. Even on Earth there is enormous variability in this respect. The likelihood is almost zero that aliens from another planet, even one very similar to our own, would match us sufficiently for successful mating to take place.

Some theorists maintain that the human race originated on a planet other than Earth. If we grant that that is what occurred, it could be that today's alien visitors come from the same planet, and are therefore of the same species as ourselves. In that case, mating would be much less of a problem. But from what we have seen of our alien visitors, this doesn't seem likely. Only a tiny percentage of all the visiting aliens are sufficiently humanlike in appearance for it to be possible that they are of the same species. If we do share a common origin, either they or we have changed so much in the past tens of thousands of years that we could no longer be taken for members of the same family.

However, there are some humans who claim from personal experience that sexual relations with aliens are possible. Elizabeth Klarer was a wife and mother living in the hills of Natal, South Africa, where she had seen UFOs on several occasions. Eventually, in 1956, she met one of their occupants. Akon, a scientist from Meton, a planet in the Alpha Centauri constellation, was seeking an Earthwoman as a mate for experimental purposes. "We rarely mate with Earth women," he explained. "When we do, we keep the offspring to strengthen our race and infuse new blood".

What began as a clinical experiment turned into a meaningful relationship:

> I surrendered in ecstasy to the magic of his love making, our bodies merging in magnetic union as the divine essence of our spirits became one ... and I found the true meaning of love in mating with a man from another planet.

She also found motherhood, for she became pregnant and was taken by Akon (together with her beloved MG car) to Meton, to bear her child there. She spent four idyllic months on Meton, where there was no pollution (except that caused by her car, presumably), everyone was vegetarian, and there were horses for her to ride once she had recovered from childbirth. Unfortunately, however, because Meton had a different vibratory rate to that of Earth, she

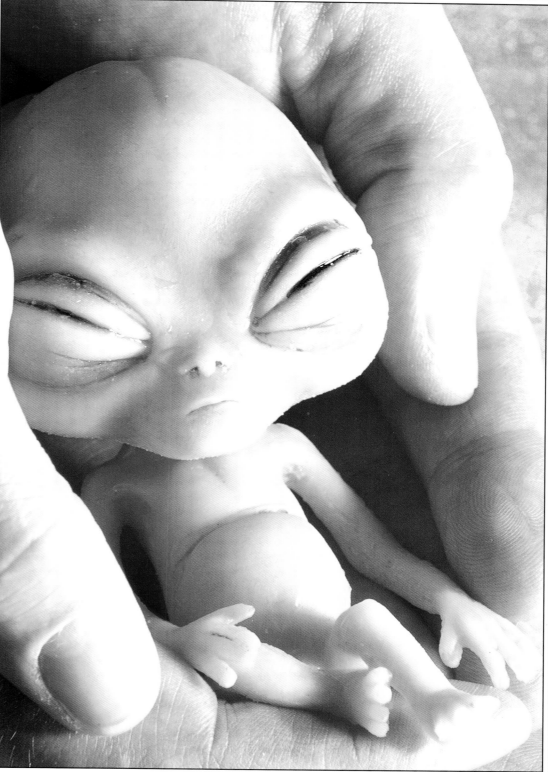

Some who have been abducted claim to have had sexual relationships with aliens. Could such trysts surmount the genetic obstacles to produce alien-human hybrids?

could not live there permanently. She had to return (together with her MG) to Africa, leaving her son Ayling to be brought up by his father.

The following year, a similar experiment was carried out, this time

between a human male and an alien female. Once again the location was an isolated rural one, but this time it was a Brazilian farmer, Antonio Villas Boas, who was the selected mate. He was working in his fields late on the night

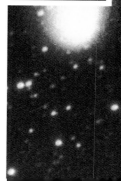

of October 15, 1957 when a UFO landed close by. He tried to get away, but his tractor stalled, presumably immobilized by the three short aliens who dragged him into their spacecraft.

There, they undressed him and rubbed a liquid over his body with a wet sponge-like object, led him into another room where a blood sample was taken, and then left him for half an hour. Some kind of gas was pumped into the room, which made him vomit. Then a woman came into the room:

> She came in slowly, unhurriedly, perhaps a little amused at the amazement she saw written on my face. I stared open-mouthed, for the woman was entirely naked, as naked as I was ... She was beautiful, though of a different type of beauty compared with that of the women I have known. Her hair was blond, nearly white ... her body was much more beautiful than any I have ever seen before. She was much shorter than I am, her head only reaching my shoulder. The woman came towards me in silence, looking at me all the while as if she wanted something from me, and suddenly she hugged me and began to rub her head against my face from side to side. At the same time I also felt her body glued to mine ... I became uncontrollably sexually excited ... We ended up on the couch, where we lay together for the first time. It was a normal act, and she reacted as any other woman would. Some of the growls that came from her at certain times nearly

Tommy Lee Jones and Will Smith starred in the Hollywood blockbuster The Men in Black, *which was based on the idea of a secret organization formed to tackle all forms of alien life.*

> spoiled everything, as they gave me the disagreeable impression of lying with an animal ... Then we had some petting, followed by another act, but by now she had begun to deny herself to me, to end the matter. When I noticed that, I too became frigid, seeing that that was all they wanted, a good stallion to improve their own stock.
>
> Before leaving, she pointed to her belly, and smilingly (as well as she could smile) pointed to the sky. I interpreted the signs as meaning to say that she intended to return and take me with her to wherever it was that she lived.

The female entity that Antonio Villas-Boas mated with seems to have been physically compatible with him, and may have been genetically so. This implies that she was of the same species as ourselves. We cannot be sure that she was of the same species as her companions, though Villas-Boas supposed this to be so. He never had a clear sight of any of his other captors, though he describes them as "men". They wore close-fitting dress which covered them entirely, and helmets twice the size of a human head with three tubes coming backwards out of them. This suggests that they had some difficulty adapting to Earth's atmosphere.

It is reasonable to suppose that the purpose of the gas which made Villas-Boas vomit when he was put in the second room was to enable the female

to function without a helmet. In other words, apart from a minor difficulty in adapting to our atmosphere, his captors were of the same species as ourselves. This makes the Villas-Boas case, consequently, very much the exception. Only very rarely are abductions carried out by beings like ourselves. The case is also exceptional in other ways. For instance, most abductees are beamed up to a spacecraft which they never see, whereas Villas-Boas was manhandled up an Earth-type ladder into a landed vessel.

There are many questions whose answers would tell us much about our extraterrestrial visitors. Was Villas-Boas' lover the same species as the rest of the crew, or could she have been created specially – an android, or whatever? He describes both her and his captors as short, but not so short that he could not copulate with her. She seemed in no doubt how to go about the act. Does this mean that the procedure is the same on her planet, or had the aliens got hold of instructional videos?

Other problems arise in another Latin American case, that of Liberato Anibal Quintero, an illiterate farm hand employed on a ranch in Magdalena province, Colombia. One night in November 1976 he returned home tired from work and fell asleep in his hammock. Not even a thunderstorm outside roused him. Then he woke, sweating and feeling strange, and hurried out of the house. In the yard

An artist's impression of Antonio Villas Boas's experience with aliens. He allegedly had sex with and impregnated a female alien.

outside, he saw an egg-shaped UFO descend from the sky and come to ground by the cowsheds, and "people" about 1.5 metres (5ft) tall came down a sort of stairway. Three of them had long hair, and looked like women.

They noticed Quintero, and overpowered him. He came to in a room bathed in light; the only other occupants were the three women, who were rubbing his back as though to relieve the pain incurred in his struggle. He responded to the caresses of the nearest woman and this led to sexual intercourse. Afterwards, she seemed to want more, and when he proved exhausted, she made some barking noises which were answered from elsewhere in the craft. A yellowish drink was brought for him, which restored his sexual energies, and something of an orgy followed. Finally, he was given an injection and came to lying on the grass, with no sign of the UFO or its occupants.

In the Villas-Boas case there was a clear indication that breeding was the purpose of the encounter. In the Quintero case it is less evident, but we must suppose that if this was a carefully planned space mission, it is unlikely that a casual sexual encounter would be permitted. We must conclude that this, too, was intentional; and if intentional, then purposeful.

The real meaning behind this mating with aliens may be disclosed by another sexual encounter, this time from North America. Sightings of UFOs had given Bruce Smith, of Oregon, a strange yearning for a relationship with a space female. His therapist suggested that this was because he was having difficulties with his Earthly sex life – he was currently going through divorce. Bruce would have liked to believe this, but one night an alien female appeared in his bedroom, accompanied by two male companions. She was 1.7 metres (5 ½ ft) tall, "not bad looking", and naked. They made love, and some time later he was taken on a mental voyage to a galactic nursery, where between 30 and 40 of the children that he saw were his.

The aliens told him that there were already either 340,000 or 34 million children – he wasn't sure if he'd understood them correctly – born with Earth fathers like himself. The

intention was that when they reached adulthood – somewhere around 2020–2030 – they would colonize Earth. With Earth fathers, there should be no legal obstacles. Bruce was delighted: "I'm proud they picked me. I've got kids in space".

THE MEN IN BLACK

Even though there is no consensus as to what aliens look like, most witnesses have no problem recognizing the beings they see as otherworldly. Villas-Boas, Quintero and Smith may have been having sex in the normal way, but they had no doubt they were coupling with an alien. Naturally, if the being was seen stepping out of a saucer, the presumption would be that it is an extraterrestrial. Even when they are

seen independently from their craft they are recognized, however. It did not cross American abductee Whitley Strieber's mind – when he was disturbed at night by intruders in his bedroom – that his home was being robbed by terrestrial burglars. Even in the semi-dark, he knew that the metre-tall (3-ft) being was neither a child or a dwarf, but something otherworldly.

However, there is one category of entity which seems to stand at the borderline. They seem to be both part of a continuing folklore tradition and a new species which might have been created specifically for our conspiracy-suspecting age: the so-called "Men in Black".

> We have been watching you and your activities. Pleased be advised to discontinue delving into the mysteries of the universe. We will make an appearance if you disobey.

Albert Bender, director of the

An artist's impression of the sinister Men in Black – aliens masquerading as official investigators into paranormal experiences.

International Flying Saucer Bureau (IFSB), had been warned, but flying saucers were his life, and he was determined to unearth their secret. So he persisted – and in July 1953 he became the most famous of all who have been privileged with a visit from the legendary Men in Black.

Despite its grandiose title, the IFSB was an amateur, one-man affair. Its headquarters were in Bender's own home, in an attic den decorated with occult imagery like a schoolboy's bedroom. But it was the height of the flying saucer boom, and his Bureau had been well accepted in the saucer community. A year after founding his organization, he felt he was in a position to reveal the truth about the flying saucers to the world. Before he finally committed himself, he felt he should report his knowledge to the authorities in Washington. But neither his organization nor the U.S. government were ever to learn his secret. Before he could mail his report, it was stolen from a locked box in his den, even though his family assured him that no one had set foot in his room.

A few days later he had the explanation. The Men In Black came calling. Bender was lying down in his bedroom after being overtaken by a fit of dizziness when he became aware that three shadowy figures had entered his room. All were dressed in black clothes, like clergymen, but wore Homburg hats which concealed or shaded their faces.

Despite their menacing appearance, the three men were not hostile. All fear left him as they started to communicate with him telepathically. After requesting him to address them as Numbers 1, 2 & 3 respectively, they confirmed that yes, he had indeed stumbled upon a part of the secret of the saucers, but he must not reveal it. Further, he was to disband his organization, cease publication of its journal, and swear not to reveal the truth to anyone. He swore to do so on his honour as an American citizen, and in return they told him the rest of the secret. True to his word – though he subsequently wrote a book-length account of the incident – Bender has never revealed the secret of the saucers.

Bender is just one of many individuals in the UFO world who claim to have been visited by the Men in Black.

One of the Men in Black who visited Albert K Bender in August 1953.

Typically, they appear in a group of three, generally male. They may arrive by car, which is likely to be a black Cadillac in the United States, or a black Rolls Royce in Britain. In either case, the model will be somewhat out-of-date, yet immaculate and even new-smelling. When Robert Richardson was visited by two MIB after a UFO sighting in 1967, his visitors arrived in a black 1953 Cadillac. He noted the number and checked it, and found that it had not yet been issued – another characteristic feature.

In appearance, the MIB conform closely to the popular image of the "secret service man" – dark suit, dark hat, dark shoes and socks, but white shirts, all crisp, clean and new-looking. They are frequently described as vaguely foreign or exotic. Often, there are more bizarre features. They walk stiffly, perform even trivial movements awkwardly, or handle familiar objects as if doing so for the first time. The MIB who in 1976 came to silence Dr Herbert Hopkins, a 58-year old doctor who had been asked to act as consultant on a UFO case, seemed to be wearing lipstick. In other respects he behaved like a poorly-programmed robot. He terminated their talk by saying, very slowly, "My energy is running low – must go now – goodbye," and walking falteringly and unsteadily to the door.

Their faces are expressionless; not hostile, but slightly sinister. They reveal little about themselves. If they produce evidence of identity, it is invariably

found to be false. In March 1967, the United States Air Force issued a memo entitled "Impersonations of Air Force Officers" specifically concerned with impostors claiming to be USAF officers checking up on UFO witnesses. What they have to say is usually menacing. After George Smyth of Elizabeth, New Jersey, had questioned some boys about a possible alien encounter, he saw two dark, slant-eyed figures watching from a parked car. Later, he received a phone call telling him to give up UFO investigation, a typical instruction.

The MIB speak in quaintly formal phrases reminiscent of Hollywood B-movies – "Again, Mr Stiff, I fear you are not being honest", or "Mr Veich, it would be unwise of you to mail that report". UFO witness Robert Richardson received a typical threat – "If you want your wife to stay as pretty as she is, then you'd better get the metal back!" In this as in many cases, the Men In Black seem to have astonishing sources of information. Somehow they knew of Richardson's encounter when only four people – himself, his wife and two senior officials of a UFO organization – knew of it.

Men in Black show many signs of unfamiliarity with human ways. Dr Hopkins' son John was visited by a stranger with a female companion who claimed to know them. The female seemed strangely built, with breasts set very low and something wrong about her hips. They sat on the sofa, pawing and fondling each other. The male asked John if he was doing it correctly, and when John went out of the room for a moment, asked his wife Maureen if she had any nude photos of herself.

Are the Men in Black human beings – secret service or security officers, agents of an international Nazi or Jewish conspiracy? Could they be aliens masquerading as humans? Are they flesh-and-blood entities, astral entities or hallucinated phantasms? All these and many other hypotheses have been proposed, and profound psychosocial theories have been advanced to account for their origin. They seem in many ways to be creatures of the imagination – direct descendants of the demons and other evil entities who have figured in popular folklore throughout human history. Yet at the same time, those who have encountered them relate the incident in such matter-of-fact terms that it seems they must be something more than fantasy.

The lone MIB who appeared to Peter Rojcewicz in the library of the University of Pennsylvania seemed human enough. He was dressed in what is standard gear for MIB – black suit, white shirt, black tie and shoes. He suddenly appeared before Rojcewicz, saw that he was reading a book about flying saucers, and asked if he had ever seen one. When Rojcewicz said he hadn't, his visitor asked if he believed in their reality. Rojcewicz said he wasn't sure he was very interested in the phenomena, and the MIB screamed at him, "Flying saucers are the most important fact of the century and you are not interested?" he then rose, put his hand on Rojcewicz's shoulder, said "Go well on your purpose," and left. Rojcewicz looked to see where he had gone and found the library totally deserted. He returned to his reading, and after a while things returned to normal.

What makes this case exceptional is that Rojcewicz is a psychologist and a professor of folklore. He sees today's UFO-related MIB as part of an on-going tradition: "part of the extraordinary encounter continuum – fairies, monsters, ETs, energy forms, flying saucers, flaming crosses". An encounter with a MIB will frequently change the witness's life. Though some are left frightened and nervous, others report that their lives have changed for the better. This appears to be true of many types of encounter with otherworldly beings.

What does Rojcewicz make of his own encounter? He doesn't think he was dreaming, but suspects he was in an altered state of consciousness. He describes the MIB as being "somewhere in the crack between real life and fantasy". With their evident association with UFO incidents, the MIB could as well be terrestrial security agents as extraterrestrial beings. But on balance, the evidence points towards the second interpretation. The many reports of their awkwardness and unfamiliarity with human ways and their uncanny access to private information seem unlikely characteristics for agents of the FBI or CIA. What we can say for certain is that,

whatever their nature, the Men In Black are truly a myth of our time. They symbolize man's age-old fear of the unknown in a strikingly contemporary guise. What remains uncertain is what kind of reality underlies the myth.

On the face of it, we would expect the occupants of UFOs to be more easily understood than any of the other categories of visitors we have considered. If they are the equivalent of our own space explorers, we should be able to share their motivations and understand their behaviour. In fact, as we have seen, just the reverse is true.

Ten years ago, it was estimated that there had been about 150,000 serious UFO sightings which could not be explained by conventional means. If we understand them aright, that means that 150,000 crews of extraterrestrials left their home planet, doubtless with considerable trouble and expense, to come visiting our planet. Why? Even after a half century of UFO visits, their nature remains ambiguous, their purpose is obscure, and even their very existence is open to question. Compared with the other beings from other worlds, they seem singularly ineffective.

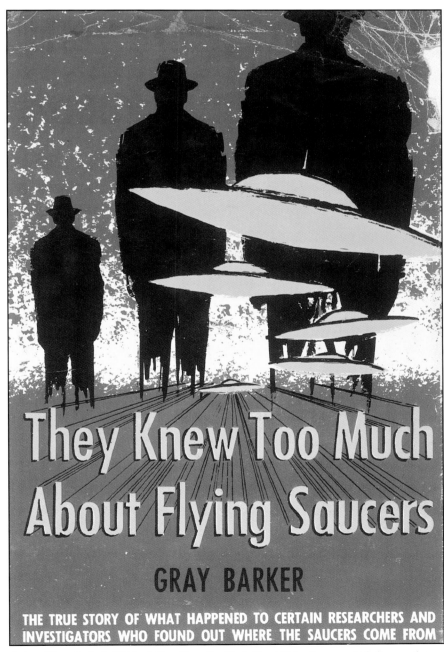

Jacket of Gray Barker's 1956 book They Knew Too Much About Flying Saucers, *which discusses the experiences of those who have been visited by the mysterious Men in Black.*

WATCHERS OF THE SKY

"Egregors are astral entities, formed from invisible vital forces, grouped in collectivities, oriented towards a single order of ideas. In nature they are colossal forces, types of giant and terrible creatures, capable of generating whirlwinds and convulsions which can shake entire countries. These are the genii of the ancients, the Watchers of the Sky of occultists, the Titans of Fable ... When they are angered, they unleash catastrophes. But they also direct the stars, protect just nations and men. They include the nine powers: angels, archangels, thrones, dominions, principalities, virtues, powers, cherubim and seraphim. They are the knights of the holy grail."

Paul Carton, a twentieth-century occultist, is one of many thoughtful scholars convinced of the existence of otherworldly beings, somehow intermediate between the gods and ourselves. These, though they are among our most frequent visitors, are the ones which make us most uneasy. The gods today are seen either as immanent beings in whom we have absolute trust, or as remote and inaccessible. We are relatively "comfortable" with the extraterrestrials because, however alien, they seem to exist on the same plane of reality as ourselves. But these other intermediate categories of visitor, neither gods nor physical beings, disturb us more profoundly. Although they evidently inhabit some other level of reality, they are not far removed from our everyday reality, and they intrude upon our lives in disconcerting and often horrifying ways ...

GHOSTS

Sightings of ghosts have been reported throughout recorded history. Millions of "ghost stories" have been told, some

Füssli's depiction of the nightmare transforms psychological experience into a visitation from a physical entity whose intentions are not benevolent.

with a shiver by the fireside on wintry evenings, others with morning-after puzzlement at the breakfast table. Although they are continually dismissed by skeptics, they persist. While fairies, leprechauns, witches, mermaids, and other such beings have largely faded into folklore, ghosts continue to be reported in all sorts of context. They are the most varied, the most persistent, of paranormal phenomena.

Most ghosts are phantoms of the

Humans abducted by demons: traditionally, artists depict benevolent entities with birdwings, while the malevolent are winged-like bats.

living, and it may seem inappropriate to be considering them in a book about visitors from other worlds. But there are a minority of ghosts who do indeed seem to come from the beyond. It may be that we should think in terms of another dimension of reality rather than of another place in the physical universe, but the spirits of the dead certainly do not inhabit our here-and-now world.

Every culture has its own ideas about what happens to us when we die. For some, it is simple extinction, for others, flesh-and-blood resuscitation. Some believe that we are reincarnated in a continuing spiral until we have earned sufficient credit as humans to qualify for admission to a higher level of existence. Some believe that at death we lose our individual identity, and are absorbed into some communal "greater being".

In this book we are not concerned with any of these possibilities. Many cultures however – perhaps most – hold that death is not the end of personal existence, but a transition from one form of existence to another. They suppose that we move on to another stage of development, as an infant moves from childhood to adulthood. The difference is that the next stage takes place elsewhere than on Earth.

If this is so, then perhaps the dead have the power to revisit Earth, and

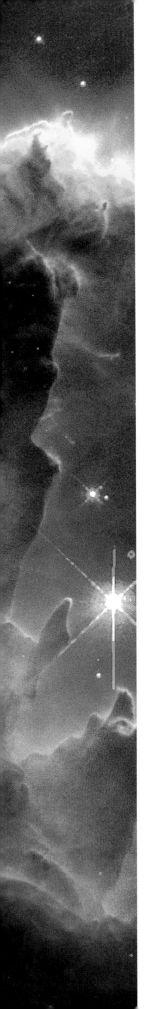

During a séance at the Paris home of researcher Delanne, a misty figure detaches itself from the medium and approaches the sitters.

witnesses to see, hear and sometimes even smell and touch.

The fact that apparitions are occasionally seen by some of those present but not by others suggests that some extrasensory process is at work. Technically, this amounts to hallucination – but hallucination takes so many forms that it is more a handy label than a precise definition.

Ghosts are sometimes photographed. If we could be confident that they are what they seem to be, this would establish that they have some degree of material presence. Unfortunately, there are only a handful of ghost photographs which merit serious attention, and even these fall short of being entirely convincing.

But even if ghosts are no more than hallucinations, something is needed to trigger the process, and if the dead survive, they may be the ones responsible. We may reasonably suppose that whatever form our future existence takes, it allows for at least a partial return to Earthly life, in something resembling Earthly form. Moreover, the dead retain their Earthly appearance and attributes, or else they resume it for the purpose of revisiting Earth, for otherwise they would not be identified.

One reason why the nature of ghosts remains unresolved even though they have been around for more than 2000 years is because – as in the case of UFOs – there has been a tendency to lump all paranormal apparitions together as though they were one single category. Despite superficial similarities, they are not. It is only recently that poltergeists have been separated as a category; perhaps we shall soon make the necessary distinction between the other three categories – phantasms, hauntings and revenants. We are not concerned here with the first two of these, because they do not come from other worlds in any sense of the word. Phantasms of the living are by definition Earthly events, and though hauntings seem to involve the dead, they appear to be spirits which are for some reason earthbound. There is an abundance of testimony that both these categories of

even intervene in Earthly affairs? This possibility has been a source of controversy among Christian theologians. On the whole, Catholic doctrine says they can, while Protestant doctrine says they can't. Many native cultures have formulated their own ideas as to how and under what circumstances the dead will return. For example, there is a widespread belief around the world that if the dead are not buried in the correct manner and with the appropriate rituals, they will be sad or angry, and return to Earth to reproach or harass their negligent relatives.

Where are they returning *from*? We Earthpeople cannot conceive of anything existing outside space and time, and so those who accept survival as a fact necessarily assume that the dead exist *somewhere*. The more sophisticated theorists have stopped thinking in terms of Valhallas and Heavens, and accept that any future existence may take place on some level beyond our imagining. Be that as it may, when the dead return to Earth, they do so in a more or less physical form. There is something seemingly material for

Edward Kelley and Paul Waring, sixteenth-century magicians, summon a spirit from the grave, hoping it will tell them where to find buried treasure.

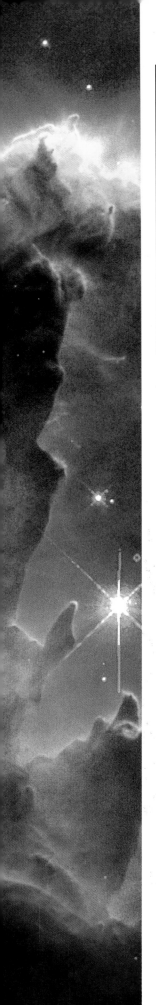

Italian scholar Marsilio Ficino added posthumous fame to his living reputation, when he appeared to his friend Mercati to honour their agreement.

ghost exist, but on what level they exist, and how they function, remain subjects for speculation.

The third category is that of "revenants". The French word, meaning returners, or "those who come again", has no equivalent in English. These are, ostensibly, the dead returning to visit the Earth where they once lived. As such, they qualify for inclusion in our survey of visitors from other worlds. The clearest examples of this type of case are "compact" cases – when an agreement has been made between two people that whichever should die first will return and tell the other. Here is a classic instance from the fifteenth century:

The scholar Marsilio Ficino, after a discussion on the nature of the soul with his friend and pupil Michele Mercati, agreed that whichever died first would try to revisit the other. Early one morning in the year 1491, while Mercati was studying at his San Miniato home, he heard a horse galloping in the street and stopping at his door, and Ficino's voice exclaiming, "Oh, Michele, what we said about the other world is true!" Mercati hastily opened his window, and saw Ficino on a white horse. He called after him, but he galloped away out of his sight. The servant whom he sent to Florence to enquire about Ficino learnt that he had died about that hour.

Clearly, though Ficino is only recently dead, he has had time – assuming "time" has any meaning there – to see enough of the "next world" to know that it does indeed exist: his visit to his friend does therefore constitute a return from another world.

In other cases, the dead person has definitely been "gone" for a considerable period. A British climber at 5000 metres (16,000 ft) in the Himalayas found himself suddenly confronted by the figures of two school friends, both of whom had been killed in a car crash several years earlier. The physical circumstances – extreme cold, oxygen shortage, fatigue – combined with the psychological stress, are sufficient for us to assume a hallucination. But that doesn't answer the question of why these particular people were chosen to play the part of the "ghosts". The climber was not consciously thinking of them. Did his subconscious mind create the hallucination, or did his dead friends make the decision to "return" to give him moral support?

These particular ghosts seem to have done nothing positive, but perhaps their mere presence was a comfort to the climber. The publisher of one of my books, Peter Dawnay, told me how once – driving alone across Spain through the night, in a great hurry to catch the ferry to North Africa – he felt certain there was someone in the passenger seat who "took control", and seemed to be protecting him from danger.

More specific were the experiences of Edith Foltz-Stearns, an American aviator whose life was repeatedly saved thanks to warnings from invisible co-pilots. At the age of twenty-six, taking part in an air race between Los Angeles and Cleveland, she was off-course and low on fuel. A forced landing was her only option. She looked for a possible place, and thought she'd found one – a stretch of railroad track. She started the descent when a girl's voice said "No, Edie, don't!" She levelled off and flew on – and minutes later she found herself approaching the runway of Phoenix airport. The voice had been that of a school friend who had been killed in a car crash years before, when she was only fourteen years old.

Most career pilots, however skillful, suffer an accident sooner or later, but Edith's professional life was accident-free. Ironically, she died as a result of injuries sustained when stepping off a bus. She was convinced she knew why – she never flew alone. When danger threatened, a deceased friend or a relative would actively help her to safety. During World War Two, she was

Extreme conditions, such as mountaineering or polar exploration, are notorious generators of hallucinations who appear as guides, companions, even protectors.

ferrying a Mosquito over the English Midlands in dense cloud when her dead father's voice suddenly cried "Edie, look out!" Without even thinking, she shot upwards – and narrowly missed a jagged mountain peak.

It is common for widows and widowers to have the illusion that their lost spouse has returned. Sometimes this is with some kind of message or even an explicit purpose, at others they are simply a "felt" presence which nevertheless, just by being there at all, gives comfort to the bereaved one. Here is a typical instance. Three members of a family – a brother and a sister living together, and a sister married and living further down the same street – all reported being visited, separately, by apparitions of their mother, who had recently died. None of the family was regarded as mentally ill, but the brother had a history of paranormal experiences, and twice saved his family from death during World War Two by predicting bomb hits.

After his mother's death, he reported seeing her:

> Her apparition comes usually twice a week through the closed door of my bedroom and stops at the foot of my bed. She stands there for a while and stares at me. I have the impression she wants to tell me something but can't.

He found the experience so frightening that he would hide his head under the blanket until she disappeared. Both he and his sister, at breakfast, would hear their mother's footsteps on the upstairs landing, and hear her calling them – but while the brother heard her call his name, the sister heard her call hers! The sister also saw her mother on several occasions, when going to sleep or waking. Like her brother, she didn't welcome the visits.

> Always I have tried to keep her out of my room, trying to push her away. But I have not felt anything to touch.

Once she asked her mother if she was happy; her mother nodded and said, "Yes".

The other, married, sister also said she'd seen her mother very often, coming into the bedroom and stopping at the bed and gazing. Like her brother, she hid under the bedclothes, but she could still see her with her eyes closed.

> Twice I woke up my husband, but Frank never could see her, though she was there, just at the foot of the bed, staring at me. He said I was just as mad as my poor mother was, and the next minute he was back asleep.

The others did not know of her experiences till some time later.

In the view of Dr Lucianowicz who reported the case, the apparitions were hallucinations, created by the witnesses as a way of expressing feelings of which they were not consciously aware. This may be so, but it does not rule out the possibility that the dead mother actively participated in the event, a possibility supported by the fact that all three saw her independently.

There is less room for doubt when something is actually *achieved* as the result of the ghostly visitation. Around 1830 a German priest, Johann Weber of Mittelberg, Bavaria, was called out one winter's night to a sickbed about an hour's walk from his presbytery. On his way home he lost his way in the snow and darkness, and strayed onto a frozen lake whose ice broke beneath his weight. Suddenly he saw a bright light coming towards him from the atmosphere. The light materialized into the shape of a young orphan boy who Weber had helped and taught, but who had died earlier that year. The apparition stretched out its hand and – with much more than a boy's strength – pulled the priest out of the water, without speaking indicated the way home, then vanished.

Next morning he revisited the scene of his accident. The broken ice and his footsteps in the snow confirmed that the event had really happened. But what of the rescuing boy? Was it the boy himself, returned to Earth to help the man who had previously helped him? Was it his guardian angel, taking the likeness of the boy? Was the apparition a hallucination produced by his subconscious mind?

Whichever explanation we find least implausible, one thing has still to be accounted for – the fact that Father Weber was really and truly rescued. That, at least, took place on the here-and-now physical plane.

In Shakespeare's play, the ghost of Hamlet's father returns to Earth because he has some "unfinished business" he wants his son to perform.

SPIRITS OF THE DEAD

Visiting the theatre today, we would be surprised if the hero of a modern drama were to receive a visit from his father's ghost. But when Shakespeare's audiences watched Hamlet speak with his father, returning from the grave in quest of revenge, they accepted it as part of the familiar order of things. It was only a short step from the "natural" to the "supernatural" – a distinction which they would not have recognized. It is only our age of science which has hung a curtain to separate this world from the next.

If interaction between the dead and the living has been taking place throughout history, so have claims by individuals that they possess a special power to facilitate such interaction. When Saul, in the Old Testament, asks the Witch of Endor to help him contact the spirit of Samuel, it is clear that he is making use of a socially established

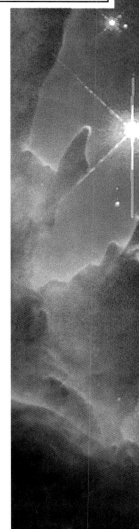

institution. In the mid-nineteenth century though, what had been a service provided by isolated individuals became a widespread movement involving neither marginal folk making a dubious living on the fringes of society nor a priestly elite performing esoteric rituals, but a collective activity in which all could take part. What happened in Hydesville, New York, in 1848, was a democratisation of otherworldly communication.

The breakthrough could hardly have taken place in more humdrum circumstances. When the home of the Fox family was disturbed by strange rapping sounds, twelve-year old Catherine Fox called out "Do as I do, Mr Splitfoot!" and found that the raps echoed her hand-clapping. This was hardly more than a childish game. But when the two-way exchange developed into a rudimentary form of what seemed to be communication with the dead, the implications were recognized. As news of the event spread, so did enthusiasm. American society, impatient with authoritative religion, welcomed the indication that two-way communication with the dead was not the exclusive privilege of saints, mystics or magicians, but a right available to one and all.

However, just as older religions had found that professional priests were a convenient interface between the populace and their gods, so spiritualism developed its professionals – individuals who seemed specially gifted when it came to contacting the dead. Though they humbly insisted they were little more than a telephone exchange, the most proficient practitioners could expect to win fame and, if not a fortune, at least a comfortable living in return for their labours.

Inevitably, a spirit of competition entered the business. Mediums vied one with another as to who could produce the "best" phenomena – that is to say, demonstrations which provided the strongest evidence that the spirits were responsible. They improved their techniques. From laboriously rapped-out messages, mediums moved on to direct-voice. It was found that if a medium let

Saul, King of Israel, asks the Witch of Endor to help him contact the spirit of Samuel: today we would call her a Spirit Medium rather than a Witch.

The spirits levitate a table to impress a visitor to the Fox sisters: such "parlour tricks" were supposed to be evidence of their supernatural reality.

herself lapse into a trance state, her body might be temporarily possessed by a "control" from the Other Side. Often, this was the spirit of a native American – such as Grace Cook's "White Eagle" – or a lisping infant – Gladys Leonard's "Feda" – with whom the medium would get on intimate, everyday terms. Speaking through the medium, the control would act as stage manager, requesting music, arranging the seating, introducing the spirits to the sitters and generally ordering everyone about.

Are "White Eagle", "Feda" and their kind really visitors from other worlds? Though some controls display considerable individual personality, many of them reveal disconcerting

lapses of memory. Leonora Piper's "Dr Phinuit" mysteriously lost his ability to speak his native French, and Professor Broad records:

> I have been asked for "the key of my wigwam" by a control who professed to be an African Negro child, and I have heard an entranced medium suggest that the sitters should sing "The Swanee River" [a Negro spiritual] to encourage a control who claimed to be a Red Indian chief.

Eileen Garrett, probably the most perceptive and intelligent of all mediums, acknowledged that she very much doubted whether her Arab

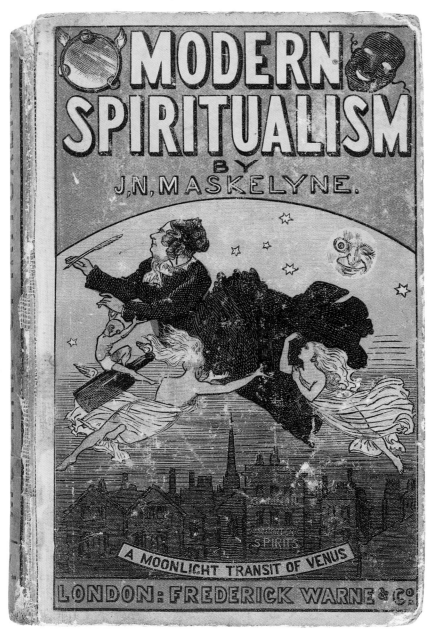

American medium Mrs Guppy flies through the night sky over northern London, borne by spirits at the bidding of sitters gathered in a distant séance-room.

objects of all kinds were appearing in locked rooms – including, on one memorable night in June 1871, the stout American medium, Mrs Guppy, who was teleported through the London skies half-clothed.

The American medium D D Home caused tables – and sometimes himself – to rise in the air. He would handle hot coals, and pass them on for others to hold, in full light and in the presence of many observers. Never once was he caught cheating. Unless we are prepared to dismiss a mass of eye-witness testimony – often made reluctantly by people who would have liked to catch him out – we must conclude that much if not all of Home's performance was genuine.

But genuine *what?* Home claimed that his ability to do these things was a gift from the spirits. There is no obvious connection between a flying table and an otherworldly spirit though, apart from the medium's say-so. Do the dead return from their future existence to perform these crude parlour tricks? Can they not devise some more effective way to prove they have survived? The trumpet-blowing, table-rapping séances were more like noisy children's parties than solemn reunions between the living and the dead. They were degrading to the spirits, and disgusted many of those who might have made a serious study of phenomena which presented a genuine challenge to science. As a result, spiritualism acquired a "marginal" label. Even the involvement of a few eminent sympathizers, such as scientist Sir William Crookes and prime minister Arthur Balfour, was insufficient to restore respectability.

Many believers, too, were dissatisfied with the evidence. The conviction gradually grew that, to be totally sure the dead were really implicated, they should be seen. Some mediums found they had the ability to cause spirits to appear, visibly, in the seance room. At first it was supposed that the dead were actually reappearing in their own bodies, but gradually investigators learned what the actual process was. The medium exuded from bodily orifices – mouth, navel, or elsewhere – a psychic substance which Nobel-laureate Charles Richet named "ectoplasm". This useful stuff could be shaped into any form, so

control "Uvani" had any independent existence. She considered he was more probably a convenient creation of her own unconscious mind.

But if that is true of the controls, what about the spirits themselves? Spoken messages are easy to fabricate. Even if they contain personal details, the medium might herself acquire the information by chance or by design. Equally ambiguous were the descriptions of the next world supplied by the dead. In the 1880s, a band of spirits gave Miss M T Shelhamer, of Cleveland, Ohio, a book-length account

of the blissful "Summer Land" to which those of us who behave ourselves can expect to go when we die – but can we trust her spirits to tell the truth?

For those who doubted, some more tangible proof was needed. This took the form of asking the spirits to prove they were "super-human" by doing things we humans can't do. By the 1860s, in séances such as those conducted by Herne and Williams in London, tables were being raised from the floor, music was being broadcast through trumpets floating in mid-air, messages were being written on slates inside sealed boxes and

A demonstration of levitation by the American medium D D Home, about 1868: on several occasions he was seen to rise to ceiling height.

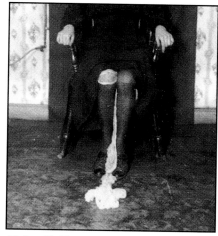

Medium Kathleen Goligher exudes ectoplasm from between her legs, around 1917: sometimes it became sufficiently rigid to support a table.

Through the agency of Florence Cook, the spirit of "Marie" appears at Hyde, c.1902: the concealing draperies are typical of séance-room appearances.

the spirits used it to make likenesses of their living selves. To all intents and purposes, the old dream of summoning the dead from their graves had become reality.

Unfortunately, there were problems. First, while ectoplasm was being produced, the medium seemed to be exceedingly light-sensitive, so all manifestations had to take place in very reduced light. Second, the ectoplasm itself was sensitive to touch, so only rarely were observers permitted to feel it, and then only very gently. Third, the medium needed to be isolated for the process to be carried out, usually behind a screen or within a "cabinet",

unwatched by others. Finally, when the materialized spirit emerged from the cabinet, it was invariably wearing long white drapery, usually with a massive turban. While it is possible that this is the normal dress in the next world – setting aside the question of why the dead feel any need to be dressed at all – it was an unfortunate coincidence that by wrapping the body so completely, only an absolute minimum of flesh was visible for identification purposes. However, it seemed to be enough, for the voluminous draperies rarely prevented sitters from identifying their deceased friends and relatives.

Clearly, such conditions lent

themselves to trickery. From the first, it had been suspected that some mediums were cheating, but so long as communication was limited to spoken messages, this could be little more than suspicion. But when walking, talking, materialized spirits made their appearance in the seance rooms, it was relatively easy for a skeptic to establish whether the alleged spirit was what it was claimed to be, or the medium (or an accomplice), suitably disguised.

One of England's most successful mediums in the 1870s was a young girl named Florence Cook, who convinced the eminent scientist Sir William Crookes that her powers were genuine. Her séances were often enlivened by the appearance of Marie, the spirit of a girl who had died at the age of twelve. Two sitters, Sir George Sitwell and his friend Carl von Buch, noted that beneath her customary long white robes, Marie was wearing a corset. If it was surprising that a spirit should wear a corset, it was particularly so for a twelve-year old spirit. One of them

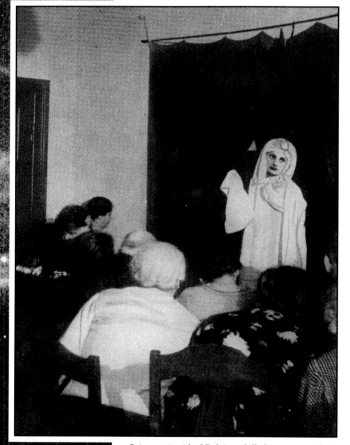

Princess Astrid of Belgium, killed in a car crash in 1935, reappears three years later at a séance with Einer Nielsen at Copenhagen, swathed in drapery.

grabbed the materialized adolescent, while the other drew the curtain of the cabinet where the medium herself should have been sitting entranced. She wasn't. Florence Cook and the spirit of "Marie" turned out to be one and the same.

Cook may have been cheating when she materialized other spirits at Crookes' home, as well. We can't be sure. But the fact is that one medium after another was found cheating in this way. Understandably, sitters demanded more rigorous tests, and the spirits reluctantly agreed to be photographed. Once again, the results were ambiguous. The cameras showed extraordinary phenomena taking place – but close-ups of ectoplasm often revealed a woven substance, very similar to cheesecloth, a fabric which coincidentally happens to be the kind most easily concealed in bodily orifices.

Furthermore, the materialized forms were often ludicrous in appearance. On May 31, 1938, the Danish medium Einer Nielsen produced a materialized form purporting to be Princess Astrid of Belgium, who had been killed in a motor accident three years earlier. Apart from the face, the entire figure was draped in robes. Not even the hands were visible. In past times, when the dead were coffined in their winding sheets, it was understandable that on their reappearance they should be wrapped in long white drapery. But by Princess Astrid's time the practice had long been abandoned, so why didn't she appear in the clothes she was buried in?

Moreover, since all mediums agreed that ectoplasm was produced only with great fatigue and suffering, it seems wasteful that they used it to manufacture clothing when it could have been used to show us more of the figure beneath. If one of the purposes of materialisation was to convince us of their identity, the spirits might have managed something better than these unconvincing performances.

There is no doubt that curious things happen at séances; but the evidence that they happen as the result of otherworldly intervention is only circumstantial. Alleged materializations such as that of Princess Astrid of Belgium are as much an insult to the dead as to the living.

OTHER WORLDLY PHOTOGRAPHS

No photographs of gods exist, and very few of such religious figures as the Virgin Mary. Quite a number of Star People – those who maintain they have come from outer space to live among earth people – have been photographed, but because they are incarnate in human bodies, they look pretty much like anyone else. Ghosts have shown themselves remarkably camera-shy. Even extraterrestrials – who as demonstrably real beings should present no problems to the photographer – have yielded remarkably few photographs. Elizabeth Klarer successfully photographed her lover's flying saucer, but when she wanted to show us what Akon himself looked like, she provided her own drawing of him. For her half-breed son, we did not even get that.

But only a dozen years after the dead began to communicate with the living, they allowed themselves to be photographed. Around 1860, a photographer in Roxbury, Mass, found a second figure on some of his plates. There seemed no other explanation than that the camera had caught what the human eye could not detect – the presence of a spirit. Soon, many others confirmed that when a medium sat in on a photographic session, spirits might manifest on the finished photo, even though they had not been visible to the eye when it was taken.

Unfortunately, faking such photographs is child's play for a photographer, and in 1874 French spirit photographer Edouard Buguet was taken to court for defrauding his clients. His guilt was manifest. However, even when he had been proved a charlatan, many of his former sitters remained convinced he had been genuine, and accused the authorities of a conspiracy fostered by the Roman Catholic church.

With so much trickery and fraud going on – not to mention unconscious self-deception – few scientists were willing to take the trouble to see whether spiritualism contained anything of value. Only a handful of people braved the ridicule and investigated the claims, forming the *Society for Psychical*

This photograph by Buguet shows the spirit of the poet Gerard de Nerval beside the sitter, a M. Dumont: a year or so later, Buguet was convicted of faking his photos.

fact remains that there is no direct evidence that they originate with the spirits of the dead, or any other otherworldly source. Two of the most perceptive and intelligent mediums – Eileen Garrett and Geraldine Cummins – both cherished doubts as to the origin of their gifts. While both clearly possessed remarkable powers of *some* kind, it is misleading to label them "spiritualist".

Today, while spiritualism is still very much alive, with millions of enthusiastic followers throughout the world, it has become a belief-system which, like any other religion, appeals to some and not to others. It has not proved to be what the first starry-eyed table-rappers of the 1850s expected it to be – the rift in the veil which separates this world from the next.

ON THE EDGE OF THE UNKNOWN

If Spiritualism is genuine, it ought to be a vital factor in the lives of us all: if false, then it and its high priests should be ruthlessly exposed, and believers in it disillusioned of a faith that is altogether vain.

The editor of *Pearson's Magazine* did not conceal his private opinion, "that every séance at which physical 'phenomena' occur is simply an exaggerated conjuring entertainment". Nevertheless, when, in his issue for March 1910, he introduced the first of four articles by William Marriott under the heading "On the Edge of the Unknown", he issued an open challenge to the champions of spiritualism to "come forward with absolutely unimpeachable evidence of genuine Spiritualistic phenomena".

Marriott, a professional magician and illusionist, had been examining the claims of spiritualism for many years, but had yet to receive any indication that they were what they claimed to be.

A hundred mediums have conjured before me, filling me more and more with amazement at the credulity of human nature, and only the most accomplished of

Research in London in 1882, and similar organizations in France, the United States and elsewhere.

What these investigators established is that, while spiritualism was riddled with trickery on the one hand and self-delusion on the other, it has also produced some truly puzzling phenomena. If we can believe the investigators and their cameras, the French psychic Marthe Béraud – though she was suspected of cheating on other

occasions – successfully produced white materializations even when her mouth was full of red fruit juice. Engineer W J Crawford photographed Belfast medium Kate Goligher's ectoplasmic extrusions in the act of raising a table. The Polish poet Franek Kluski caused monstrous animal forms – including a large living bird – to materialize in a small locked room.

But even though these and other phenomena remain unexplained, the

William Marriott with the "spirit forms" he used in his demonstrations of spiritualist fraud: in a darkened room these absurd figures deceived many.

them giving a performance that would have mystified an intelligent child.

He had attended many séances, and on several occasions successfully exposed the deceivers. But he did not stop there.

> I have gone farther than merely establishing, to my own satisfaction at any rate, the fact that materialisations at séances are produced by fraud. I myself have produced the same effects – also by fraud, or perhaps I should say, by purely physical means.

Whereupon he found – as many debunkers have found – that he was supposed to have mediumistic powers himself.

> Avowed Spiritualists who have seen these spirits of my own production have frequently refused to believe that I was not a medium. Only by displaying the apparatus by which the materialisations were brought about have I convinced them that my spirits were merely due to exaggerated conjuring tricks.

At one séance, the medium retired into a curtained cabinet, whence a luminous spirit form emerged. With the aid of a luminous globe, he was identified by the sitters as "King Draco". Meanwhile, the mischievous Marriott surreptitiously slipped into the cabinet where, of course, the medium should have been sitting entranced. For obvious reasons, the medium was *not* in the cabinet; in a short while, however, the spirit form returned:

> As the form entered the cabinet, he sat down on what he thought was the settee. It happened to be my knees. As my arms went round him, he gave a yell followed by language which I will not repeat. My friend had the light up in a moment. And there for the faithful was the edifying sight of the medium, clothed in flimsy white draperies, struggling in the arms of myself! His wife shrieked out that we had murdered her husband, and came to his rescue. Fortunately, she was restrained by some of the others present.
> Our money was hastily returned to us, and the party broke up in an excitement that bordered on hysteria on the part of some of the believers. On visiting the house next day, I found that the birds had flown. Mr and Mrs X had vanished into thin air; though, as I afterwards found, they contrived to keep in touch with some of the circle, who still maintained their faith in these incapable charlatans.

Marriott was particularly astonished that such eminent and otherwise intelligent persons as Sir William Crookes and Sir Oliver Lodge found the evidence convincing. The most brilliant of the founders of the Society for Psychical Research, F W H Myers, had died in 1901. It was not long before a number of mediums claimed to receive messages from his surviving spirit. One of them was Rosina Thompson, who had known and worked with Myers during his lifetime. She gave two sittings to Lodge, at which communications ostensibly from Myers came through.

But when Lodge asked, "Do you want to say anything about the Society?" Myers, its most prominent member, replied, "Do not think I have forgotten. But I have. I have forgotten just now". Later, he remarked that he had also forgotten his mother's name. Marriott commented:

> To Sir Oliver Lodge, this sitting was "as convincing as anything that could be imagined of that kind." To me, and surely to all unbiased persons, it is as unconvincing as any alleged phenomena could possibly be.

But he kindly lets them off the hook by adding:

> The great point is this: they did not know how the "phenomena" could have been caused by trickery – in other words, they did not know what to look for … Scientists, however eminent, are emphatically not the people to investigate these matters … The scientist who sits where he is told to sit and looks where he is told to look is the ideal subject for the wiles of the conjuror or the medium, and before him effects can be brought off that would be impossible before an audience of schoolboys.

His comments on Crookes were particularly perceptive, when he wrote:

> Brilliant as he is in investigations where chemical precision and insight only are required, he proved himself totally unable to make any allowance for the human equation. His experiments with Florence Cook illustrate this fact. They took the form of materializing séances, at which a spirit called Katie King appeared. She was photographed on several occasions, and Sir William wrote: "Katie never appeared to greater perfection, and for nearly two hours she walked about the room, conversing familiarly with those present. On several occasions she took my arm, and the impression conveyed to my mind that it was a living woman by my side, instead of a visitor from another world, was so strong that I asked her permission to clasp her in my arms. Permission was graciously given, and I accordingly did – well, as any gentleman would do under the circumstances.

"Spirit hands" are credited with many séance-room phenomena: Marriott shows how a clever "medium" can provide himself with as many helping hands as he needs to perform his wonders.

Marriott commented:

Exclamation marks, italics, and all the stereotyped forms of wonder would be wasted on this amazing revelation. Sir William, after walking and talking with a young woman for two hours; after holding her in his arms and presumably kissing her; after emphasizing the strength of his impression that she was a living woman, still prefers to believe not that she was a mundane being in collusion with the medium, but that she was – a spirit!

He concluded his investigations more in sorrow than in anger:

If I am one of the "scoffers", it is not because of any original bias, but because of the arrant humbug, cheap trickery, and pathetic self-delusion that I have encountered at every point of my investigations of Spiritualism, and I combat its teachings because I believe them to be in defiance of the soundest of all laws – those of common sense and human experience.

Such exposés throw doubt on the validity of much ostensible communication with the dead, but it was a 1972 experiment which demonstrated the mechanism by which plausible spirits might be created. The "Philip" experiment was carried out by a group of Toronto researchers, who deliberately created a fictitious historical personage who gradually took on a semblance of life of his own. The imaginary Philip not only produced physical phenomena like those produced by "real" spirits but provided a good deal of information about himself!

While the success of the Toronto experiment does not prove that *all* ostensible spirits of the dead are in fact constructed by the subconscious minds of the living, it does demonstrate that it is a viable alternative to the idea that they are coming to us from other worlds.

CHANNELLING

Many who have been fortunate or unfortunate enough not to have face-to-face encounters with extraterrestrials have, none the less, enjoyed contact of a different kind in the form of "channelling", whereby they receive messages from extraterrestrial beings, generally when in a trance state.

Again, this is nothing new. From the Old Testament prophets onwards, there have been people claiming to receive communications from otherworldly sources. The coming of the saucers gave a new impetus to the channelers simply by suggesting a new category of communicators. Scores of people – virtually all of them American – began to receive messages from extraterrestrial entities. These are much the same as the messages given to those who have personal encounters with alien visitors, but since the channeler is sitting in his own cosy home instead of being out at night on a lonely mountainside, his messages tend to be wordier – much, much wordier.

For example, in the 1950s a young lady named Pauline Sharpe began to receive messages from an entity named Nada Yolanda, who in turn was able to pass on messages from – among others – Jesus Christ and Christopher Columbus. Pauline learned that in a previous

The vision of an angel appears before Abraham to bring him the news that he will become the Father of Sons.

appeared in the doorway of her living room and spoke to her. He revealed himself to be Ramtha, a former Earthperson – originally from Mu, but living in Atlantis – now residing in another dimension. Knight was a child of his long, long ago (actually 35,000 years ago, give or take a year or two). He made contact with her by coming around her body in the auric field, and working through the seals or chakras – though what this meant in biological terms was not explained. He revealed that we ourselves are God, and offered such timeless wisdom as "you are rich if you are happy in your soul, for gold cannot buy happiness". In the 1980s, he announced that

> President Reagan will lead the American government till it's like Solon's in ancient Greece and in so doing give the country back to the people.

Not all communicating entities are so far removed from us in time. Bernie King is an electric engineer, formerly of Mojave, California, who since his earthly death in 1974 has been:

> residing on a Space Ship, along with several hundred other Beings who are dedicated to the preservation, and, if you will, the salvation, of the Planet Earth.

Fortunately his wife Beti is a psychic, and through her he sends informative messages and answers questions about other planes of reality. He has met Jesus twice, but does not see him often, as he is working on a different project. On the other hand, Eisenhower, Robert Kennedy and Gandhi are among his team-mates, and the volunteers include many showbiz people including Louis Armstrong, Tommy Dorsey and Nat King Cole. Thanks to the purer environment, Bernie's fingernails grow less fast, and he does not need to shave at all, since "whiskers on your planet are an environmental result".

Generally speaking, the question of whether these channeled communications are what they seem to be is not a vital one to society at large. If that's how people choose to spend their weekends – and their dollars – that's their business. From time to time however, they lead to social consequences which make it a

incarnation, she had agreed to carry out a mission on Earth, in which she would act as a "female polarity". During the early years she employed automatic writing; since 1960, she

> speaks the words aloud as she receives them through mental telepathic impression or electro-magnetic beam from higher dimensions and from interdimensional and interplanetary spacecraft.

These are generally tape-recorded and subsequently transcribed. Volume after volume of these messages have been published. In *Visitors from Other Planets*, we learn how a crew of 2353 extraterrestrials have come to Earth in a city-size spaceship to stimulate and train us for the New Age of Aquarius, scheduled to commence around the end of the twentieth century, but apparently running late.

Most of these books consist of "teachings", but occasionally the Yolanda experience comprises deeds as well as words. She is sometimes able to visit the spacecraft above the Earth. What happens is that her Etheric Self conveys her physical body up into the ship "like an envelope, from which the real Self could slip in and out". She has not only spoken with Jesus, but actually visited with him on many occasions.

Though it is possible that channels like Yolanda gained financially from the groups they set up in connection with their messages, it is the new generation of channelers who have made it big business. In 1987 Jach (sic) Persel, who acts as channel for an entity named "Lazaris", charged $275 for a weekend course which attracted 400 to the Los Angeles Hilton. Even after deducting hotel expenses, there must have been a tidy sum left over from the total take of more than $100 000.

Currently, the most popular channeler is J Z Knight, through whom an entity named Ramtha is able to share his wisdom with us. She was joking with her husband one Sunday afternoon in 1977, in their home near Tacoma, Washington, when a "being of light" matter of importance that we establish what's really going on.

In 1975, a couple naming themselves "The Two" announced that they were "about to leave the human level and literally (physically) enter the next evolutionary level in a spacecraft", and invited others to share the undertaking, which was named Human Individual Metamorphosis. When some 20 people were reported missing, the police investigated and identified the couple as former music teacher Marshall Herff Applewhite (then aged forty-four) and one-time nurse Bonnie Lu Trusdale Nettles (forty-eight). Other names they took were "Nincom" and "Poop", "Tiddly" and "Wink", "Winnie" and "Pooh", but it was as "Bo" and "Peep" that they captured the headlines.

Without going into too much tiresome detail, they gave the impression that though they appeared in the likeness of Earthpeople, they had graduated from other planets – Bo from one planet, Peep from another. At the height of their popularity, they may have attracted a thousand people to share their experience. Many gave up all their possessions and abandoned their families; there were angry confrontations with distressed relatives. Some of the followers, too, were dissatisfied. One made the revealingly naive comment "I have to blow the whistle on these two. I'm not saying I don't believe in people from outer space, but these two are spacy. They have to be stopped".

In the end, they stopped themselves. In the summer of 1997, a comet passed within visible distance of Earth, and for some inscrutable reason, many came to believe that it carried within its tail a mighty spaceship. Applewhite and his followers – Nettles had died in the meantime – obtained instructions to board the spaceship; this they were to do by relinquishing this Earthly life. Their mass suicide made headline news. Though the event was widely described as a "tragedy", there is no indication that it was so for those most intimately involved. On the contrary, they probably died very happy people.

Another recipient of channelled messages was Marion Dorothy Martin, who in 1949 was told by her extraterrestrial contacts that the destruction of the world was imminent,

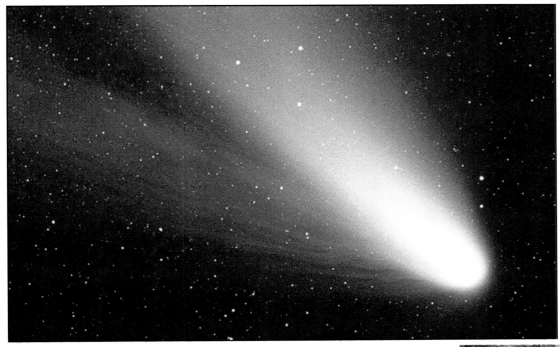

For more than 20 years, Applewhite and Nettles – "The Two" – and their followers awaited a summons from their alien contacts: in 1997 they believed a comet was the signal.

but that those who "believed" would be rescued. Several people were convinced. Dr Charles Laughead gave up his post at Michigan State University and dedicated himself to spreading the warning, issuing press releases about the forthcoming event, and inviting would-be evacuees to join their group. Others left jobs and homes, broke family ties, and joined Mrs Martin in waiting hopefully for rescue.

Sociologists from the University of Minnesota, who took the opportunity to observe the motivation of those who don't merely receive channeled messages but positively act on them. They were able to see what happened "when prophecy fails" – when the promised flying saucers failed to show up on the appointed day to ferry the believers to safety on some other world. Since the announced catastrophe never took place either, the non-appearance of the rescue-ships did not matter too much – apart, that is, from the effects on the lives of those concerned, their relatives and friends.

Channelling is significant for our study, because it shows clearly how a well-established practice – of people serving as mediums or channels for otherworldly messages – can be adapted to suit the prevailing myth. Once, such messages came from the gods; later, from the spirits of the dead; today, from extraterrestrials.

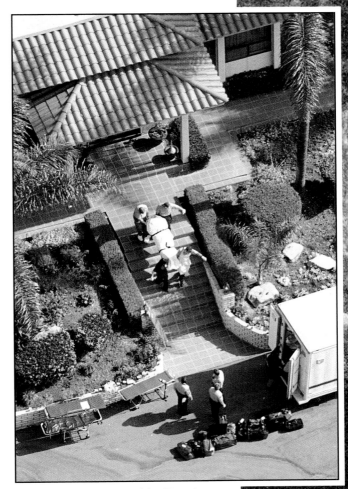

In 1997 thirty-nine members of the "Heaven's Gate" cult committed suicide, believing they would be taken aboard the spacecraft following the comet.

INDEX

Picture Credits

About the Author

Hilary Evans is an acknowledged authority on UFOs, extra-terrestrial experiences and the paranormal. He writes and lectures on anomaly research, psychical research, folklore and myth, and related subjects. He is a member of the Society for Psychical Research, the American Society for Psychical Research; the Society for Scientific Exploration; the Association for the Scientific Study of Anomalous Phenomena and the Folklore Society. He has written books on many aspects of anomaly research, notably *Intrusions*; *Visions, Apparitions and Alien Visitors*; *Gods, Spirits, and Cosmic Guardians*; *Frontiers of Reality*; and *Alternate States of Consciousness*. He is the author of four books on UFOs: *UFOs, the Greatest Mystery*; *The Evidence for UFOs*; *UFOs 1947–1987* and *UFOs 1947–1997* and has published many articles on these subjects. He was also writer–consultant for *Almanac of the Uncanny* and several other Reader's Digest publications. He lives in London.